"Before you embark on a journey
of revenge, dig two graves."

—Confucius

Sweet ❧ Carolina
MYSTERIES

Sweet Carolina
MYSTERIES

A HARD PILL
⋙ to ⋘
SWALLOW

Elizabeth Ludwig

Guideposts

Sweet Carolina Mysteries is a trademark of Guideposts.

Published by Guideposts
100 Reserve Road, Suite E200
Danbury, CT 06810
Guideposts.org

Cover and interior design by Müllerhaus
Cover illustration by Bob Kayganich at Illustration Online LLC.
Typeset by Aptara, Inc.

This book was previously published under the title *A Hard Pill to Swallow* as part of the *Miracles & Mysteries of Mercy Hospital* series.

ISBN 978-1-959634-76-8 (hardcover)
ISBN 978-1-959634-78-2 (epub)

Printed and bound in the United States of America
10 9 8 7 6 5 4 3 2 1

Chapter One

OCTOBER DRIFTED LAZILY INTO CHARLESTON. It didn't roar in on a gust of freezing rain or piling snow. There weren't surprising cold fronts to shock the color from the trees. There was merely the slightest dip on the thermometer and the fluttering of the pages on Anne's calendar to mark the seasons. That didn't mean, however, that she couldn't enjoy the creamy spice of pumpkin-flavored coffee on her tongue.

Sighing gratefully, she blinked through the steam rising from her cup to take another careful sip, the Monday morning newspaper rustling between her fingers.

"Anything interesting?" Her husband, Ralph, nodded toward the paper then set his own mug on the table next to a heaping plate of bacon and eggs. Lifting one brow, he held out a slice of bacon.

Though it smelled delicious, Anne shook her head. "No, thanks. Already had some." She laid the paper aside and nudged it toward him. "And not to spoil anything for you, but no...there's nothing interesting."

"Mmm." Ralph crunched the bacon and reached for the paper anyway. After swallowing the bite, he said, "I figured the police would have a lead on those muggings by now."

"Me too, or at least I hoped so." She pinched her lips together to stop a troubled sigh. "I just can't get over it. Three attacks, and all of them literally happened right outside the hospital. Wouldn't you think someone saw something?"

Ralph shrugged as he reached for the saltshaker. "Winter is creeping up on us. The sun sets earlier and earlier. By eight o'clock, it's way past dark."

"True." Anne shrugged off the unsettled feeling in her stomach and finished her coffee then carried her cup to the sink for a quick rinse before placing it in the dishwasher. "Will you start that before you head to the hospital?" She gave a nod toward the cupboard. "Soap is under the sink. I know it's low, but I'll swing by the store after work and pick up more."

"No problem. I'll take care of it."

"Thanks, honey." She pressed a kiss to her husband's cheek, the woodsy scent of his aftershave familiar after forty years of marriage. "Love you."

"Love you too."

Plucking her car keys off a mirrored shelf, Anne shifted her thoughts to Mercy Hospital, where she served as a volunteer and where Ralph ministered as the chaplain. Talk along the halls the last couple of days had centered around the incident that took place three nights ago. A woman from HR had been walking to her car when a shrouded figure appeared from nowhere and knocked her over the head. Fortunately, she was fine, aside from a slight concussion. Still, what the person was after was unclear since the rumor circulating was that nothing had been stolen, just like the first two muggings.

Could they even be called muggings if nothing was taken?

Anne pondered the question as she slid into her parking space at the hospital. Though the sun already peeked over the tallest gable and warmed the red brick walls to a fiery orange, she couldn't help but look over her shoulder as she made her way inside. The idea of someone lurking in the shadows made her nervous. And angry.

"Morning!"

Anne startled at the cheerful voice greeting her from the direction of the gift shop. Joy Atkins's eyebrows lowered in a perplexed frown. "Are you all right?"

Anne shivered and jammed her car keys into the pocket of her smock. "Fine. Got the jitters, is all."

Joy snorted, a sound that only she could make dignified. "You and me both. It's delivery day, so I had to get here early to unlock the back door. I was jumpy as a cricket until the van showed up with my flowers." She rubbed her slim shoulders. "I sure wish they'd figure out who's behind these attacks and what they're after so we could all get back to normal."

Anne grunted her agreement, checked her watch, and then motioned toward the back room of the gift shop, where Joy made coffee. "Do you have a pot on? I've got time for a cup before I need to start stocking inventory."

"Of course I do. I even bought some of that pumpkin spice creamer you like."

Though she'd already had a cup, Anne's mouth watered at the thought of a second helping of her guilty autumn pleasure. "Thanks."

Joy's blue eyes sparkled as she motioned her in. "So it's inventory again today, huh? Aurora still mad at you for skipping out on work and nearly bringing down the entire volunteer organization?"

"Addie was sick, and Lili couldn't get her. Besides, I was out one day," Anne protested, reaching for a cup dangling from a hook behind the coffeepot. On the front it read, COFFEE FIRST... TALK LATER, a fitting sentiment for this particular morning. "But Aurora was really upset, which is strange, because she's not usually like that."

"It's your own fault for being so dependable." Joy's Texas drawl and playful smile softened the teasing. She opened a small fridge under the counter and thumped a bottle of creamer next to Anne's elbow. "If you were sporadic and untrustworthy, you wouldn't have this trouble."

A slow grin spread over Anne's lips as she reached for the creamer. "Okay, okay. I get your point."

"Hmm." Joy snagged a second cup from the hooks and poured herself some coffee. "So, speaking of the muggings..."

"Were we still talking about that?"

"We are now." She replaced the pot and laced both hands around her cup. "I've been thinking. This last one happened on the south side of the hospital. Do you suppose the mugger hid behind the row of hedges that grows there and that's why no one saw anything?"

Anne fingered the handle on her mug while she thought. "It would be a good spot, I guess. The hedge is tall enough. But wouldn't that mean the mugging was planned and not some random, spur-of-the-moment type thing?" Somehow, the thought made the act all the more menacing. She shook her head and took a hasty sip from her cup. "Anyway, I'm more than happy to leave all that to the police."

"I suppose." Joy's tone said the opposite.

Anne lifted an eyebrow. "The police and security team have everything well in hand. There's no point in the two of us getting involved."

"Make that the three of us." Evelyn Perry joined them in the gift shop and pointed to the coffeepot. "Anymore in there?"

Joy moved aside with a wave. "Help yourself."

"Thanks. Is that pumpkin spice?"

Anne nudged the sweetened creamer toward her. "So you heard what I said? And you agree that we're just fine letting the officials handle things?"

"That's usually best." Evelyn screwed the cap onto the creamer and ambled with her cup to a small table in sight line with the door. Anne and Joy followed. Evelyn took the stirrer out of her mug and laid it on a napkin. "Unless...you know...we actually have a reason to get involved."

"Please don't let that be foreshadowing." Anne shot a glance heavenward. More often than not of late, mysteries like this one tended to get tossed into their laps. "I've got my hands full helping Lili get Addie acclimated to third grade."

Joy scraped a chair out from the table and sat. "Is she still having trouble with her new teacher?"

Anne shrugged. "I'm not so sure it's the teacher. I think Addie just misses her mom. I guess we both thought we'd see Lili more now that she's home from deployment, but those evening classes she's taking really eat up her time and energy. Of course, with our history, I don't dare say too much, even though things are definitely getting better."

Evelyn placed her hand over Anne's warm fingers. "I'm glad they have you."

Anne smiled at her gratefully. "Thanks."

"You know what you need?" Evelyn crossed to the door and yanked a paper flyer off the glass. "Exercise."

For several seconds, Anne simply stared. Next to her, Joy sat frozen as well, her cup halfway to her mouth. Finally, they looked at each other and broke into laughter.

"I need *what*?" Anne asked, gasping.

"I mean it." Evelyn's gaze bounced between the two of them. Waving the flyer in their faces, she added, "It's a well-known fact that exercise helps relieve stress. And with the hospital now offering free fitness classes to staff, it's the perfect opportunity."

"Wait…what?" Anne grabbed the flyer and flipped it over to read. "When did this start?"

"You haven't heard?" Joy set her cup down and tapped the back of the sheet with her finger. "It's a new employee benefit Garrison is trying out to improve morale."

Evelyn nodded. "Exactly. Like I said."

Anne returned her gaze to the flyer. "Yoga, low-impact aerobics, strength and conditioning, CrossFit…" She read the list of instructors, then lifted her head. "Basically, a little bit of everything."

"Yep. I was thinking about checking out the low-impact aerobics." Evelyn leaned forward eagerly. "You gals wanna join me?"

Torn with indecision, Anne bit her lip. An exercise class could be fun, but… "I'm not sure. We keep Addie pretty late, and by the time we eat and help her with her homework—"

"That's only on Monday, Wednesday, and Friday while Lili's at class. What about Tuesdays and Thursdays?" Evelyn insisted.

"We could even throw in a Saturday morning sometimes," Joy added. Anne's brows rose, and Joy lifted both hands, palms out. "I'm not saying we have to, just that it's a possibility."

"Hmm." Anne thought a moment longer and then agreed with a slow nod. "I guess it wouldn't hurt. It could be a good distraction."

"Speaking of distractions…" Joy angled her head toward the door hospital administrator Garrison Baker had just stepped through. "We should thank him for coming up with the idea."

Anne would have agreed, except that Garrison seemed to be making a beeline straight toward them, a frown on his lips and his brow creased with lines of worry.

"There you are," he said to all of them in general. "I was hoping I'd find one of you. Have you heard from Shirley?"

"Shirley?" Anne glanced at her watch. "Is she here? I know she's been taking on some extra shifts, but I didn't think this one started for another hour."

Garrison's eyes rounded and he looked them over, one by one. "You mean…you haven't heard? She didn't call you?"

"About what?" Evelyn demanded. "What's going on?"

Garrison ran his hand through his hair. "Shirley put in some extra hours on her last shift…"

A feeling of foreboding crept over Anne, shooting her pulse into overdrive. "Spill it, Garrison. What are you talking about?"

She didn't think it possible, but the lines on Garrison's brow actually deepened. "It happened last night," he said at last, blowing out a breath. "After she got off work, Shirley was mugged."

Chapter Two

IMAGES OF SHIRLEY BRUISED AND bleeding flashed through Anne's brain. Though her mouth was dry, she managed to stammer, "Is—is she all right? Was she hurt?"

"Where is she? Why didn't she tell anyone?" Evelyn's words piled over Anne's in a rapidly rising flood that forced Garrison's hands up.

"I only talked to her for a minute. The attack happened outside of the parking garage. Shirley claimed she was fine—a little shaken up but otherwise okay."

She was okay. A tiny bit of tension seeped from Anne's tight shoulders.

Joy jerked her cell out of her pocket, punched some buttons, and then held the phone to her ear. After a moment, she frowned and ended the call. "Straight to voice mail."

Anne reached for her purse. "I'm going over there."

"Aurora is expecting you." Joy shook her head. "I'll go."

"You can't leave the gift shop." Evelyn stood. "I'll check on her." She looked at Garrison. "You coming?"

"Of course. Give me two minutes to clear my schedule."

At Evelyn's nod, Garrison took off at a brisk walk in the direction of his office.

"Unbelievable. Four attacks in less than a month." Arms crossed, Evelyn directed a troubled glance at Anne and Joy. "Why do you suppose Shirley didn't call one of us?"

"I'm sure it was late by the time she finished with the police." Joy's fingers fluttered over her mouth and chin. "Maybe she didn't want to worry us?"

An anxious sigh blew from Evelyn's lips. "Lotta good that did. We're more worried now than if she'd just called."

Anne couldn't have agreed more. Spying movement, she craned her neck to see over Evelyn's shoulder then widened her eyes. "There's Shirley." She waggled her finger toward the entrance doors. "She's coming in now."

The words were like catalyst to a fire, mobilizing all three of them into action. Shirley backed up a step as she spotted them rushing toward her. "Whoa now. I take it you talked to Garrison?"

Anne's gaze traveled over Shirley from head to toe. No bandages circling her forehead. No slings or casts. She was dressed in a fashionable rust-colored sweater that complemented her brown skin. Jeans. White tennis shoes. She looked completely normal and nothing like the victim of a brutal attack at all. No doubt she, Joy, and Evelyn had looked like the three furies storming out of the gift shop, ready to dispense retribution on whoever had dared harm their friend. But here was Shirley, appearing unhurt and calmer than any of them felt.

Anne took a deep breath and reached for Shirley's hand. "Are you all right?"

Her mouth turned upward in a weak smile. "I'm fine. Tired from not getting any sleep last night, but otherwise okay."

Taking her cue from Anne, Joy clasped Shirley's other hand. "I wish you'd called one of us."

"I would have, except Mama was in a state by the time I got home. It took me over an hour to calm her down enough to go to bed. After everything that happened, I was so exhausted, I just crawled under the blankets with her, though it was another hour before she finally fell asleep." She blew out a shaky breath. "I wouldn't have even come in today except I told Seamus McCord I'd visit the security office and review the surveillance footage."

"There's footage of the attack?" Evelyn's pitch rose with excitement.

Though Anne would have liked to continue clutching her friend, Shirley pulled her hands free and shook her head. "Not of the attack. Seamus just thinks there might be a clue in the video footage from the Grove. I think he's hoping I'll see something that might spark a memory."

None of which made the slightest bit of sense if the attack took place outside of the parking garage as Garrison had said. Anne gestured toward the gift shop. "Can you sit for a minute and tell us what happened?"

Shirley agreed and allowed herself to be led to a chair near the gift shop door with just a slight tug on her hand. That was the first clue she wasn't quite as "fine" as she claimed. The second was when she accepted the cup of coffee Anne brought to her with shaking fingers.

"Thanks." Closing her eyes, Shirley took a sip. "Mmm. I'm gonna need more of this stuff if I want to get through this day."

Joy jumped to her feet. "I'll put on another pot."

"You're sure you're okay?" Evelyn asked, pushing to the edge of her seat as Joy swished away.

"To be honest, I'm a little shaken up." Shirley shuddered and set her cup on the table. "And I'm worried about Mama. She must've mumbled Jesus's name a hundred times in her sleep last night."

Poor Regina! "She was afraid for you," Anne said.

Shirley nodded.

"Let's pray for her peace of mind right now," Evelyn said.

She reached for both of their hands and led them in quiet prayer. When they opened their eyes, Joy had rejoined them. She added her own amen as she sat down.

"So? What exactly happened, Shirley? Did you see who attacked you?"

"Unfortunately, no. The person came up from behind me. Hit me over the head with something hard before I could get a look. I'm not even sure if it was a man or a woman."

"They hit you on the head?" Alarm clawed its way up Anne's throat and made her voice shrill.

"It's a goose egg, that's all," Shirley soothed, patting her hand. "I'll probably have a headache for a day or two and be right as rain before the week is over."

"But you did get checked out, right?" Joy's eyes widened with concern.

"I did. And I promised Mama I'd get looked at again today, just to be sure I'm okay."

"That's good. It'll give us all some peace of mind." Evelyn shuddered and wrapped her arms around Shirley's shoulders. "Goodness, sweetheart, I'm so glad you're safe."

"Me too." Shirley blinked several times then swiped her finger under her eyes and sniffled. "Anyway, it all happened after I left the hospital."

"What time was that?" Anne asked.

"Must have been just after eight or so. I grabbed my purse and sweater out of my locker and headed toward the parking lot, but then I ran into one of the other nurses in the hall and we chatted for a little bit before I went outside."

Evelyn leaned in closer. "You didn't see anything unusual? Nobody hanging around who was acting out of the ordinary?"

"Not at all." Shirley reached into her pocket and pulled out her phone. "I heard a message ding and glanced at the screen to see who had texted me."

"Oh, Shirley." Anne's chest tightened. Distracted people made easy targets because they weren't cognizant of their surroundings.

"I know. I promise, I only glanced at it for a second. But that's all it took, because the next thing I knew, I was facedown on the sidewalk with a whopper of a headache."

"So, no sign of your attacker." Joy's words were more of a statement than a question.

"Not even a glimpse."

"And nothing was taken?" Evelyn asked.

"Not that I could tell. Of course, I was pretty rattled last night, but I looked through my purse again this morning. Far as I know, everything is still there."

"What about your badge?" Anne's mind raced as a flicker of an idea took root. "Maybe whoever attacked you didn't want money. Maybe they were trying to get access to certain parts of the hospital."

Joy caught on to her train of thought immediately. "You mean maybe they were after drugs?"

"Could be, right?" Anne asked quickly. "Someone broke into one of the Pyxis machines just recently."

"Sorry, girls."

Anne's excitement deflated as Shirley held up her badge.

For a second, no one spoke, and then Anne said, "Okay, they weren't after cash and they didn't take your badge, so what did they want?"

"I wish I knew." Shirley replaced the badge in a pocket of her purse and then slid the strap over her shoulder. "For now, I need to get moving. Seamus is expecting me."

"Wait." Joy hurried to the back of the store and returned with a to-go cup clutched in one hand. "Take this with you. And call one of us after you've had a chance to talk to Seamus."

"What about Regina? Do you want someone to sit with your mom?" Evelyn asked.

"Dot was with her when I left, but if it looks like I might be here a long time, I'll give one of you a buzz." She patted the phone-shaped bump in her pocket.

"We'll keep our phones on and close by," Anne said, wrapping Shirley in one last hug before releasing her toward the elevators. Once the metal doors closed her from sight, Anne let out her breath in a whoosh. "I'm so glad she's okay."

Evelyn frowned. "Me too, but it could have turned out very differently."

"You're right. Things could have easily been much worse," Joy added.

"I think we all know what that means." Anne's gaze passed from Evelyn's somber stare to Joy's. Both women nodded, their jaws set in similar determined lines.

Anne lifted her chin and said what all three obviously felt. "We've got work to do, ladies. The three of us are going to figure out who is targeting the Mercy Hospital employees."

Chapter Three

ANNE SLUNG THE STRAPS OF her tote bag over her shoulder and stepped out of the hospital elevator. After a mind-numbing day taking inventory yesterday and again today, she was tired, covered in dust, and looking forward to spending a little time doing something other than checking items off spreadsheets.

Down the hall, Joy and Evelyn waited outside the entrance to the fitness studio where Garrison had set up free classes for hospital staff and volunteers in an effort to improve morale. Surprisingly, Shirley was with them, and she was already dressed in a pair of yoga pants and a loose-fitting T-shirt that had the name of a famous Christian band stamped on the front.

Anne sucked in a breath and hurried over. "What are you doing here? Did your doctor say it was okay for you to exercise?"

Shirley pressed her fingers to the injured spot on the back of her head. "I know, I know, I should be home resting. But I don't have a concussion, so he said I'm free to do anything that feels good. I promise I'll do a light version of the class and not be too strenuous." Her eyes narrowed as she slid her gaze over her friends one by one. "Plus, if I know y'all, you three have already started plotting how you're going to figure out who's behind these muggings. Am I right?"

Shirley always knew what they were up to. Refusing to look at the other two, Anne swallowed guiltily. "Well, of course we'll help out if we can."

"Mm-hmm." Shirley wagged her finger at them then started for the door. "Come on then. Might as well burn off some calories while we talk about it."

"No point in trying to hide it from her," Joy whispered as she turned to follow.

"I heard that," Shirley called over her shoulder. She let her own bag slide to the floor next to the wall, then tapped her toe while she waited for the others to gather around. "So? What have we learned so far?"

"Not much." Anne grimaced and dropped her tote next to Shirley's. "After work yesterday, I went to the south side of the hospital to scout around, but I didn't find anything I thought might be interesting."

"And I checked outside the parking garage." Evelyn plopped onto a stool to kick off her shoes. "Where exactly did you say your attack took place?"

Shirley gave them the approximate location then grabbed Evelyn's bag and handed it to her. "Honestly, I hardly ever park there. Normally, I look for a space inside the garage." She frowned. "Don't know what inspired me to change my routine. Maybe if I hadn't, I'd have seen something on the video footage."

"If you hadn't changed your routine, watching video footage might not have been necessary, because you wouldn't have been attacked," Joy said gently. "You were in the wrong place at the wrong time, that's all. Nothing you could have done about it."

"I suppose you're right." Shirley nodded toward the entrance as several people began trickling in. "Looks like we're not the only ones taking advantage of this class. How long has it been going on?"

"A couple of weeks now." Anne watched a handful of people file in then dipped her head toward one of them. "Isn't that Garrison's secretary?"

Shirley craned to look then nodded. "That's Julie, all right."

"Good afternoon, ladies!"

Anne took her gaze from Julie and turned toward the front of the class where a very fit young woman in snug-fitting athletic gear bounced on her tiptoes. "Thank you all so much for coming today. I'm Talia Reynolds, and I'll be your instructor. If you haven't already changed, the dressing rooms are over there." She pointed toward the back of the studio then checked the time on a brightly colored band on her wrist. "We'll get started in about ten minutes, so fill your water bottles, grab a mat, and let's get ready to burn some calories."

"Wow." Joy ran her hands slowly over her hips. "I hope this class makes me look like her."

Anne snorted a laugh. "Oh please. You look fine."

"Exactly. I look fine. *She* looks amazing."

"She certainly looks fit." Evelyn finished tying her shoe and stood. "And young. Now scoot, you old nanny goat. You're going to need time to wriggle out of those clothes."

Joy chuckled good-naturedly as she edged toward the dressing rooms. Since Anne had changed in the volunteer locker rooms, all she had to do was stow her bag, which she did in a row of cubbies along one of the walls. Above the cubbies were shelves lined with yoga mats and lightweight dumbbells. A couple of people reached for the three- and five-pounders, Garrison's secretary among them. Anne figured lifting her feet would be enough of a workout for this first week of class and settled for a mat to do stretches on, as did Shirley. Anne smiled at Julie, who paused to chat when she saw her.

"Anne, so good to see you."

"You too." Anne tucked the rolled-up mat under her arm then shook Julie's hand. "This is really nice. Please let Garrison know I appreciate him organizing the class, especially now, with everything that's been going on."

"I sure will." Julie's reddish-brown ponytail swung as she shifted her weight to her other foot. "It's crazy what's been happening, huh?" She tipped her head toward Shirley. "I heard Shirley was one of the victims. I'm glad she's okay."

"Me too." Anne adjusted the mat then angled her head curiously. "So, still no leads on who's behind the attacks at the hospital?"

The cheerful look on Julie's face dampened as she sucked a breath between her teeth. "Oh, I'm not sure I should talk about…"

"Of course. Sorry. I just thought maybe you'd heard something you could share."

"Um…" Talia, the instructor, ducked into Anne's line of sight. "I'm sorry, did I hear you say something about an attack at the hospital?"

Anne pivoted her stance to include Talia. "Julie and I were just talking about the muggings."

Talia's face did not register any recognition, so Anne pressed on. "You know, the one that took place night before last and the other three earlier this month?"

Still nothing.

Finally, Talia shook her head. "I'm sorry, I've been so busy getting material ready for this class, I guess I haven't been paying attention to anything else."

Since they still had a couple of minutes before class started, Anne filled her in with a summarized version of events.

Talia listened quietly, her dark eyes round with worry. "How terrible. Does stuff like this happen often in this part of town? They sure didn't tell me that when I agreed to come on board."

"It's very unusual," Julie piped in quickly. She dropped her gaze, bit her lip, and then continued, "Well, I mean, it does happen, but not more than in any other city."

"She's right," Anne seconded. "Charleston is a wonderful place to live, and our law enforcement works really hard to keep it safe."

The concerned lines around Talia's lips said she wasn't convinced. "Well, I sure hope they catch whoever's responsible. My classes go late. Normally, I won't get out of here until after eight." She glanced hopefully at Julie. "Do you know if the hospital plans on implementing extra security?"

"I'm not really sure," Julie admitted. "I could check for you, if you want."

Anne cleared her throat. "The hospital has always maintained a top-notch security team, even before any of this started. I'm sure they'll take whatever precautions are necessary, but you could always ask one of the guards to walk you out if you're worried."

Talia tugged on the end of her ponytail while she thought and then nodded. "Yeah. Maybe I'll do that." She motioned toward the front of the room. "Well, we'd better get started."

As she moved away, Joy eased over to join Anne and Julie. "What was all that?"

"She's worried about leaving the hospital alone after class," Anne said.

"Well, she has every reason to be concerned." Joy turned to Julie. "Maybe the hospital should think about adding security around the parking garage until this is sorted out."

"That's what Talia said. Garrison *has* mentioned it, but I don't know if it's gone any further than that."

"At least he's considering it," Joy said.

Julie nodded. "He sounded pretty confident the board would agree to pay for the added security, especially under the circumstances. I'll ask him when and if that will be happening and put something out on the hospital message board."

Feeling slightly better, Anne smiled. "Thanks, Julie. Hopefully, a couple of extra guards will be enough to deter any more attacks," she finished, just as Talia called for everyone to line up for class.

Flashing one last smile at Julie, Anne took her mat and spread it out between Evelyn and Shirley. While they stretched, Anne told them what Julie had said about the possibility of added security.

"That's good news," Shirley said quietly, but she didn't meet Anne's gaze. Was there more troubling her that she *hadn't* said? Anne didn't have a chance to ask, since Talia moved quickly from stretching to low-impact cardio, a workout that—while designed to be easy on the joints—still left Anne short of breath and with an elevated heart rate.

"Whew! That was good," Evelyn said when it ended. She wiped a towel over her red face and the damp tendrils of silver hair clinging to her neck. "Honestly, I didn't think I was working that hard, but I will definitely feel this in my legs tomorrow."

"Me too." A smile split Shirley's face. "I saw you and Joy take a breather halfway through."

Evelyn swatted her with the towel. "You just wait until you're our age."

"I'm hardly a spring chicken," Shirley replied.

The humor in her voice was good to hear. Anne took a moment to soak it in, then gestured toward the front of the room where Talia was packing up her equipment. "Our instructor was asking about security around the hospital. She sounded a little worried to leave the building alone after her last class is over. I'm going to go give her the names of a couple of the guards I think would be happy to escort her out."

"Good idea." Evelyn nodded then looked at her watch. "Say, anybody feel like grabbing a bite to eat? I hear that new grill place over on King Street is pretty good."

"I'm game," Joy said quickly.

"Not me," Shirley said. "I need to get back and check on Mama so she doesn't worry."

"Oh, right. Do you want one of us to go with you?" Evelyn asked.

"No need. Y'all go ahead and enjoy your supper. I'll tag along next time. I'm tired anyway. I'll probably hit the sack early."

Evelyn nodded and then turned to Anne. "What about you? Wanna come?"

Stomach growling, Anne nodded. "Ralph is working late. I'll text him and see if he wants me to pick something up for him. Give me a sec to talk to Talia, though."

She held up one finger. At Evelyn's and Joy's nods, she told Shirley goodbye and then hurried over to catch Talia.

"Hey, thanks so much for the class. I really enjoyed it," Anne said.

Talia straightened, a mat in one hand and weights in the other. "You're welcome." Her smile was almost instantaneous. "I'm glad you liked it."

"I also wanted to follow up on the security guards we were talking about." Anne grabbed the blocks Talia had been using to demonstrate some of the stretching techniques and followed her toward the storage shelves. "I'm sure any of them would be glad to help, but we're pretty good friends with a couple in particular. I could give you their names if you want."

"That'd be nice." Talia stowed the equipment then bent to withdraw her phone from her gym bag. "Let me just..." She swiped through a couple of the screens and looked up at Anne. "Okay, go ahead."

Anne gave her the names then waited while Talia typed them in. That done, she replaced her phone then fingered the thin leather strap of a necklace resting against her collarbones. Hanging from it was a beautiful piece of green sea glass shaped like a seahorse, with brown glass beads on either side. Anne lifted her gaze as Talia spoke.

"Thanks so much for the info," she said. "I don't know that many people here at the hospital, so this will really help."

"You're very welcome—" Anne began, but cut off when Talia gasped, her gaze fixed to something over Anne's shoulder.

"Um..." Anne turned to see the janitor emptying the wastebasket. "Is everything okay?"

"Fine." Talia yanked a jacket out of her gym bag and threw it around her shoulders. "That guy just makes me a little nervous."

Nervous? Anne frowned. "Mind if I ask why?"

"Just stuff I've heard. Do you know him?"

"His name is Benny Pierce. He's new, I think." Anne took a second look. Benny had a long nose, thinning gray hair, and blue eyes that could be called penetrating, but he'd always seemed pleasant enough. She glanced back at Talia. "Has something happened?"

Talia still watched Benny, her fingers clutching the edges of her jacket tight. "Not really." She gave a small shudder then reached for her bag. "Anyway, I hope you and your friends will come back again soon. I'll be offering different classes every day this week."

"Will do. Thanks again," Anne said.

Talia nodded, but she was already hurrying away. Even so, she seemed unable to resist tossing a glance in Benny's direction before disappearing into the changing rooms.

"Ready?" Evelyn closed the distance to stand at Anne's elbow.

"Yeah, I am."

Benny had finished emptying the trash and now opened a fresh bag with a snap. Anne turned her back to him slightly and motioned to Evelyn.

"Hey, do you know that guy?"

She looked and then shook her head. "He's new, right?"

"I think so."

Evelyn shrugged. "What about him?"

Anne bit her lip then quickly lowered her gaze when Benny's head turned in their direction.

"Nothing. Let's get Joy and go," Anne said.

She grabbed her tote and walked with Evelyn toward the exit. Fingers of apprehension scurried over her spine as they shuffled past Benny. He was done with the trash, yet he hadn't moved from the door. In fact, Anne felt his gaze on her back as if he watched them until they passed out of sight.

Curiosity, perhaps? Or maybe he'd sensed that they'd been talking about him? Either way, Anne knew one thing for certain.

She intended to learn a lot more about Benny Pierce.

# Chapter Four

ANNE LIFTED HER NOSE AND sniffed at the savory scents wafting through the doors of the Magnolia Grill. Steak. Barbecue. Baked potatoes. Her stomach rumbled in response. She pressed her hand to her middle and closed her eyes. "Mmm. I really want a steak."

"Why not?" Evelyn elbowed her playfully, popping Anne's eyes open. "We need protein—we worked out. And you can always order veggies with it."

"True." Anne resisted the urge to lick her lips as she reached for the gleaming brass handle on the door. It took a moment for her eyes to adjust to the dim interior, but once they did, she stared in appreciation at the elegantly papered walls and tasteful decor. "Nice. I'll have to bring Ralph back here sometime."

"Name, please?"

Anne turned to the hostess, a slim woman in a tight-fitting black skirt and matching blouse. "It's Mabry."

The woman jotted the information on the open book in front of her. "And how many will there be tonight?"

"Three."

She nodded, grabbed the clip-on mic attached to her collar, and said, "Table for three?"

She listened through her headset a moment, then grabbed three menus and stepped out from behind the hostess stand. "Follow me, please."

"Wow. Swanky," Evelyn said as they moved past a marble-topped bar into the dining room.

"Hush." Joy giggled, grabbing Evelyn's elbow and shoving her forward. "Anne, tonight, she's with you."

"You got it." Taking her friend by the arm, Anne said, "C'mon, Evs. I'll try not to embarrass you."

Evelyn pretended to clown, then quickly straightened when she bumped into another patron headed in the opposite direction. "Ooh...sorry." She stopped and looked from the tall, slender blond she'd hit to the man standing alongside her. "Oh hi, Dr. Seybold."

"Evelyn, hello." His gaze passed over Anne and Joy admiringly. "Who are your pretty friends?"

*Um...*Anne tightened her lips and fought the urge to flash her wedding ring. She didn't know Dr. Seybold personally, but the way he was looking at her and Joy made her feel very similar to the steak she'd been contemplating earlier. And what about the woman clinging to his arm? Didn't he care that she looked as though she were choking on a bit of gristle? Her face was pale, her knuckles white, and she fidgeted as though she wanted to bolt.

She stuck out her hand to the young woman. "I'm Anne Mabry. These are my friends Evelyn Perry and Joy Atkins."

"Kristen. It's nice to meet you." She shook Anne's hand but didn't make eye contact, then immediately returned to clutching Dr. Seybold's arm.

Poor thing lacked confidence and probably thought she could find it by dating a handsome doctor.

Stop it.

Anne mentally chided herself for forming hasty judgments and pasted on an encouraging smile. "So, how was the food?"

"Wonderful," Dr. Seybold said, glancing to his date. "You should try the prime rib. It's amazing."

"Prime rib. Got it. Thanks." She glanced at Evelyn and Joy then motioned to the hostess waiting to lead them to their table. The restaurant was busy, and her patience was likely wearing thin. "We should probably get going."

"Oh yes." Evelyn smiled at Kristen. "Nice to meet you."

"You too."

After nodding to Dr. Seybold, Anne followed the hostess along with Evelyn and Joy to a table next to a window overlooking downtown. It was brightly lit this time of year with orange and white bulbs twinkling from the bushes and nearby palms. Behind these, lights shone from a thousand office windows, reminding Anne that while the sun had set, it was still early.

"Will this be all right?" the hostess asked.

"Perfect," Anne said, echoed by Evelyn and Joy. They slid into their seats, and then Joy reached for the menus lying at the end of the table.

"Now, who was that man we just saw?" she asked.

"His name is Marcus Seybold," Evelyn said. "He's one of the cardiac surgeons at the hospital."

"A surgeon. Hmm." Joy flipped open the menu then paused. "Wait…is he the one with the nickname—"

"Uh-huh." Evelyn held up her hand to stop her from actually saying it. "He's the one. He earned it by his constant philandering."

Anne frowned. "What?"

She nodded. "He and his wife divorced several years ago. Back then, the rumor was he hated being tied down. Wanted to 'spread his wings,' so to speak."

"And by spreading his wings, you mean dating girls half his age, like Kristen," Joy said.

Again, Evelyn nodded. "I don't care for his type. Fortunately, I don't have a lot to do with him. It's the nurses on his floor I feel sorry for. I've heard he's a relentless flirt."

"Well, he is handsome, in a Robert Redford kind of way," Joy said.

Evelyn reached for her water and took a sip. "That's a good comparison. He's blond like Redford, though I would say a little more tanned. Who looks like that in October?"

"Tanning bed, maybe? I don't know him, but he seems like the type who'd spend a few hours there," Anne said. "He was very...tidy."

Actually, he was downright glossy—from his perfectly shined shoes to his immaculate slacks and a shirt that was oddly free of wrinkles. Did the man even sit during dinner?

Evelyn unrolled her napkin and laid it across her lap. "Doubtful. Did you see his tan line?" She ran her fingers across her forehead. "It was that weird kind, like he got it from wearing a cap or something."

Ah, a chink in the armor. Anne folded back the cover on her own menu and ran her gaze over the many cuts of steak and chicken.

"Enough about him. I'm starving. Do either of you know what you're going to order?"

"You mean you're not getting the prime rib?" Evelyn teased.

Anne snorted a laugh and kept reading.

Joy pushed her menu aside without looking at it. "A grilled chicken salad for me." Meeting both Anne's and Evelyn's gazes, she said, "What?"

A salad, when the restaurant smelled like this? Anne lifted her nose and sniffed deep. "Well, I'm getting whatever that smell is. Probably a steak." She glanced at Evelyn. "But I'll split a baked potato with you?"

"Perfect, but only if we get the condiments on the side so I can add lots of butter and sour cream." Evelyn set down her menu, and when the waitress arrived, they gave their order.

"So about the exercise class." Anne looked across the table at her friends. "What did y'all think?"

"It was good. Talia did a great job of keeping it entertaining," Joy said, reaching for her water glass.

"I agree." Evelyn ran her hands down her thighs. "I didn't realize how hard I was working, but I'm already starting to feel it. I bet I'll be sore in the morning."

"Me too." Anne laughed and kicked her foot out from under the table to stretch her calf. "I'm glad we went with the low impact. Can you imagine what her high-intensity classes are like?"

"No kidding." Evelyn joined in her laughter. "So what was all that at the end of class?"

"You mean about Benny?" Anne asked.

Evelyn nodded.

Anne explained what happened and then added, "What do you suppose Talia's heard that would make her nervous around him?"

"Well…" Joy bit her lip and picked at the end of her straw.

Anne turned her attention to her. "You know him?"

She shoved the straw into her glass, the ice inside clinking. "I know about him. People were talking in the gift shop a couple of days ago. Apparently, he has a bit of temper and he was heard getting into it with one of the nurses."

"But that wouldn't be enough to make Talia uncomfortable, would it? Unless she's actually seen his temper firsthand?" Anne suggested.

Evelyn scratched her finger along her jaw. "Or maybe she's heard the rumors too. And if she has a history of dealing with someone like that, who knows? Could be some PTSD acting up or something like that."

"Hmm. True." Anne took a drink. After a hard workout, the water tasted good. "Anyway, we've got our hands full figuring out what happened to Shirley. Anyone have any ideas?"

Evelyn rubbed her palms together then leaned forward to rest her elbows on the table. "Let's start by looking at the three—" She broke off and shot a glance around the crowded restaurant. "I don't really like using the word *victim* to describe Shirley."

"Me neither, but it fits, as much as I hate it," Joy said.

Anne felt as if a weight had been applied to her chest. She fidgeted then forced her thoughts in another direction. "Who was the first person to be attacked? Do either of you know her?"

"Her name is Crystal Thompson. She works in Human Resources," Joy said.

"So, right off the bat, we can cross off nursing as something the two have in common," Anne said.

"Maybe it's the hospital?" Joy suggested. "Someone with a grudge against Mercy itself? All four of the victims are employees."

Intrigued, Anne leaned forward. "Ooh, that's interesting. Maybe they're upset with the treatment they or a loved one received there."

"Or it could just be convenient," Evelyn said. "It's common knowledge that people come and go from a hospital at all hours of the night and day."

"Yeah, but in this case, all of the attacks happened shortly after eight o'clock." Anne frowned. "Why that time?"

"Good question." Evelyn leaned back to make room for the waitress who'd arrived with their food. Anne's mouth watered as the smell of grilled steak wafted from the plate set in front of her. Even Joy's salad looked delicious with plenty of ruby tomatoes, fresh carrots, and red cabbage.

Once everyone had their food, Evelyn asked the blessing then picked up her fork and resumed. "As we were saying, why eight? For all of the attacks to take place then, it must have some kind of meaning. So what's so special about that time?"

"It's worth looking into," Anne said, giving a nod to Joy as she skipped the butter for her potato, added a small dab of sour cream instead, and took a bite.

Evelyn poured a bit of sauce onto her plate then cut off a bite of her steak. "Let me do some checking. Maybe I can find something worth digging into." She brought her fork to her nose and inhaled deeply. "Mmm…like this steak."

Laughing, Anne reached for her napkin. "Okay, okay. I can take a hint. Enough talking. More eating."

That said, the conversation turned to lighter things, like Joy's recent date with Roger Gaylord at the Black Fedora Comedy Mystery Theater, but Anne couldn't help but ponder what they'd discussed as she drove home, a takeout box with a steak inside for Ralph on the seat next to her.

None of the victims had been robbed. So what had happened at eight o'clock to make someone angry enough to target the hospital? Several answers ran through her brain, but one possibility actually made her shudder.

Maybe the attacker wasn't just unhappy with the hospital. It could be something far worse. Like...maybe they'd lost someone they loved there. And if that were the case, were random employees enough to sate anger that deep or a pain that excruciating?

She didn't think so. Which led to another question, this one more chilling and somber...

Just how far would this person go to have their vengeance?

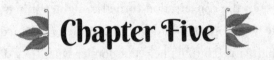

Chapter Five

Shirley slipped out of the door to Garrison's office just as Anne arrived Wednesday morning. Instead of her usual smoothed-back style, Shirley wore her hair in loose ringlets around her face, a look she wasn't free to enjoy when she was on duty. It made her look soft and pretty. And since she was coming from Garrison's office, Anne couldn't help but smile and wonder if it was intentional.

"Oh hey, Anne." A smile bloomed on Shirley's face, one as joyful and exuberant as ever, and Anne was a little surprised by how relieved she was to see it.

"Morning, Shirley." She looked her over from top to bottom. Under her jacket, Shirley wore jeans and a frilly white sweater, not scrubs.

Shirley laughed and held up her hand. "I'm off duty. The doctor won't release me for that until I've been cleared for PTSD. I just stopped by to chat with Garrison."

"Good. You could use a few days off, and I'm sure your mom doesn't mind having you home with her." Anne pointed to Shirley's head. "How's the bump?"

She touched the spot and shrugged. "Almost gone." The strange look returned to her gaze, one distant and thoughtful, but she shuddered and blinked it away. "Anyway, I should be good as new in no time."

Concern bubbling up from her belly, Anne stretched out her hand. "Shirley, are you okay?"

The smile returned and with it, an impish twinkle appeared in her eyes. "I'm great. Like my grandpa used to say, 'better than I deserve.'"

"Uh-huh. Well, just don't push yourself too hard. The job will still be here when you get back."

Shirley crossed her arms and feigned a scowl. "And now you sound like Mama."

"Who I've always said is a very wise woman," Anne fired back.

She chuckled then pushed her hands into the pockets of her jeans. "So, how was dinner last night?"

"Awesome. I think you'd like that place. We'll need to go back once you're feeling better."

Shirley moved away from the door so they weren't blocking the path if anyone wanted to go in. "Sounds good, but how about the attacks? Did y'all figure anything out?"

Anne recounted their conversation then concluded with, "What bothers me most is the idea that whoever is behind these assaults could be out for revenge."

Shirley's brows rose. "Revenge…how do you mean?"

Anne stepped closer and lowered her voice. "Well, since it's not the job connecting you to the other victims, we assumed it was the hospital. Maybe the person is angry because someone they love was injured or died while in our care."

Shirley fell silent as a FedEx driver left the elevator and strode toward Garrison's office, a rapid delivery envelope clutched in one hand.

"That's a real possibility," she said. "Some people cope with loss by finding someone to blame for it." She drew her purse strap higher on her shoulder. "Well, I suppose I'd better get home and check on Mama. Did I tell you she hasn't been sleeping well since the attack?"

Anne shook her head.

"Yeah. I think it's because she's worried something will happen to me. I keep assuring her I'm fine, but it'll probably be a while before she believes me."

"I'll be praying for her then."

"Thank you." Shirley shifted topics. "You girls gonna go to Talia's class again this afternoon?"

Reminded of the sore muscles that had scolded her loudly when she got out of bed that morning, Anne grinned. "Ralph agreed to sit with Addie after school, so I'm gonna try. You know what they say… the best cure for stiffness is—"

"More exercise." Shirley gripped her elbow with the opposite hand and pulled it across her chest. "That's what I keep telling myself." She half turned toward the elevator. "See ya this afternoon."

"Tell your mom hi for me."

"Will do."

When the elevator closed Shirley from sight, Anne turned back toward Garrison's office. The FedEx driver was just leaving and held the door for her as she stepped inside. Garrison's secretary, Julie, wasn't at her desk, but she leaned in the space between her office and Garrison's, the envelope the driver had dropped off in her hand.

"We got *another* letter from Preston Winder." Her tone said this wasn't good news. "Do you want to see it, or should I just forward it to the attorney?"

From inside his office, Garrison's voice rumbled. "I suppose I should take a look."

Julie promptly disappeared through the door. Left alone, Anne slid into one of the leather chairs along the wall to wait.

"How many letters does this make?" Garrison asked. "Three? Four?"

"Five." Even with the space between them and the door that was only half-ajar, Julie's sigh sounded troubled. "Poor guy. I remember how diligently the doctors and nurses worked to save his son's life, and how hard the Winder family took it when he passed. I know this is a pain for the hospital to deal with, but I can't help but feel sorry for him, ya know?"

Realizing that neither Julie nor Garrison was aware of her presence, Anne cleared her throat loudly and stood. In seconds, Julie popped back into the office.

"Oh, it's you, Anne." She relaxed, her shoulders dropping from where they'd risen near her ears. "Can I help you with something?"

"Actually, I'm here to see Garrison. Is he available?"

"Of course, Anne. Come on in," Garrison called. He appeared in the doorway and held out his hand.

"Thanks, Garrison. And you too, Julie." Anne smiled at her as she joined him in his office. "Thanks for seeing me."

"No problem." Leaving the door ajar, he motioned to the chairs across from his desk. "What can I do for you?"

He slid the envelope delivered by the FedEx driver into a drawer then sat and leaned forward to rest his elbows on the desktop.

"Well, I wanted to talk to you about Shirley." She motioned toward the door. "I passed her a second ago. She looked good."

"Yeah, she was just leaving."

"Really, what I wanted to discuss is the attacks." She backtracked and started again. "Of course, Joy, Evelyn, and I are concerned because Shirley was one of the victims. We've been racking our brains trying to see if we can come up with some kind of connection between her and the others, starting with Crystal Thompson. I was going to talk to her, but she hasn't returned to work since the attack and I thought maybe you could help."

"Me?" Garrison looked a little surprised by her words. "I'm not sure how. I don't know Crystal, other than the few dealings I've had with her through Human Resources."

"Oh…I thought…well, I guess I just assumed you worked closely with her since you have input on new hires."

He nodded and laced his fingers over his stomach. "That's true, but Crystal is fairly new to her position. Just over a month, in fact."

"I didn't realize that."

"Uh-huh." He leaned forward, and his gaze took on a playful gleam. "Now, can I ask you a question?"

Garrison could be charming when he chose. Over the last few weeks, Anne had seen that side of him more and more. "Of course."

"When you say you've been 'racking your brain,' I hope that's all you've been doing." Every trace of teasing faded from Garrison's face, replaced with lines of concern. "So far, we've been lucky, but this person, whoever he or she is, could be far more dangerous than we realize. I know you want to help Shirley, but I think the best thing you could do for her would be to keep yourself and others safe.

We've staffed the hospital with more security guards to escort employees to their cars at the end of each shift."

This was "hospital administrator" Garrison talking and not the easygoing man Anne had begun to see outside the hospital with Shirley.

"I completely understand your concern," Anne said. "And you can rest assured we won't do anything foolhardy."

He studied her a moment, then relaxed into his chair. "Good. I'm glad to hear it."

Compelled to add to her statement, Anne lifted one finger and said, "But…"

He stiffened. "Yes?"

She shifted in her chair to lean forward. "Garrison, Shirley is—"

All of the adjectives she could use to describe her friend flashed through Anne's brain. Precious. Loved. Irreplaceable.

The last one hit hard. She swallowed the knot that rose to her throat and started again.

"Shirley means a lot to me. I know you realize that, so I'm sure you won't be surprised when I tell you I intend to do anything I can—within reason, of course—to help figure out what's been happening around the hospital and keep anyone else from being hurt."

She choked on the last part, and her heart pounded. What was wrong with her this morning? Why was she so emotional?

"Anne."

She blinked as Garrison pushed forward to cross both arms on the desk.

"I'm as concerned as you are and will make it my business to get to the bottom of this. Shirley is a strong woman. She won't let this keep her down for long."

Forcing a stiff smile, she rose. "Thanks. I'll keep in touch, let you know if I find anything."

"I appreciate that."

Pausing to stretch her sore muscles, she laughed and said, "And by the way, I really appreciate those fitness classes you've implemented, but I may need to scale back on how many times a week I go. That Talia looks sweet, but she packs a strong workout."

At the mention of Talia, the concern on Garrison's face deepened. He straightened and tugged at his tie. "I'm glad you're taking advantage of the class. I've heard good things, which is encouraging."

He stopped, lips clamped, as though to keep anything else from spilling out. Sensing he'd said all he would, Anne turned to go. But how would she know what was bothering him if she didn't ask?

"Garrison—" She paused as the phone rang.

He rested one hand on the receiver but didn't pick up. "Yes?"

The phone rang a second time. Anne shook her head. "Never mind. I'll talk to you later."

She waved, and he nodded and picked up as she slipped out the door. Well, so much for her idea that he might be able to help her pinpoint a common denominator between Crystal and Shirley. It'd been a long shot anyway.

Anne swung her gaze around the empty outer office. Once again, Julie wasn't at her desk. Maybe she'd gone on a break. Anne scribbled a quick "thank you" on a sticky note and stuck it to her computer screen before heading out into the hall. Spying Julie a few feet away, Anne reconsidered the note and went to say goodbye in person.

"It's just not fair that they passed me up again. I have more years of experience."

Realizing Julie wasn't alone, Anne froze.

"You're a good employee, Marilyn," Julie soothed. "The hospital is lucky to have you."

She shifted sideways, giving Anne a view of the woman she was talking to. Marilyn Dodson. Anne recognized her from a few hospital functions they'd attended together. Normally, she seemed like an even-keeled person, and never showed too much emotion, but not today. Her mascara was smudged as though she'd been crying, and her lips were turned in an unhappy scowl. But it was the fury in her eyes that drew Anne's attention.

"Well, maybe you could tell that to HR, because right now, I promise I'm thinking about—" She swiped down with her hand, a chopping motion that sent the clipboard in Julie's grip flying.

She broke off and shifted her gaze to Anne. A split second later, Julie turned to see what she was staring at.

"I'm so sorry. I didn't mean to interrupt," Anne said, watching as Julie retrieved her clipboard.

Marilyn snagged a tissue out of the pocket of her scrubs and pressed it to her nose. "I should be going anyway. I'll talk to you later, Julie."

"Oh, please don't go." Anne looked at Julie. "I was just planning to say thank you and let you know I was leaving."

"No problem," she said, but Marilyn had already spun away, her white tennis shoes squeaking on the polished floor.

"Thanks again, Julie. See ya," she called over her shoulder.

"See ya," she echoed, waving to Marilyn's retreating back.

"I'm really sorry," Anne repeated. "I did just want to say thank you."

"It's okay." Julie shook her head. "With Marilyn, it's usually one thing or another, though this time, I think she has a legitimate beef." She sighed and then motioned toward the office. "Were you able to talk with Garrison?"

"Yes." Anne hesitated. "Just out of curiosity…you and Garrison were discussing a letter when I arrived. It sounded like maybe it wasn't the first one?"

She nodded. "It's from Preston Winder."

The name didn't ring any bells. "Do I know him?"

"Probably not." Julie pressed the clipboard to her chest. "His son was a patient here a little over a year ago."

"Uh-oh." Anne thought back to her conversation with Shirley. "He wasn't happy with the treatment his son received?"

"More than that."

She paused, and a feeling of foreboding sent chills running down Anne's spine.

"He passed away," Julie continued, lowering her voice to a whisper. "Preston Winder's son died at Mercy Hospital, and he's been making threats against the hospital ever since."

Chapter Six

"Preston Winder's son died at Mercy Hospital."

The words played like a drum, over and over, inside Anne's head throughout the day. She knew what it felt like to lose a child. Though it had been thirty-one years since she and Ralph lost Ariane, it still struck her sometimes, especially in October when the anniversary of her passing neared. No wonder Julie had said she felt sorry for him.

"His son was a patient here a little over a year ago."

A second line added to the cadence in her mind. Anne slid the door closed on the supply cabinet she'd been inventorying and closed her eyes. The timing was certainly right, but was it a stretch to think that Preston might be their culprit? Other people had lost loved ones in that time. It was a sad and simple fact of life at a hospital. And why target Shirley? Or Crystal or any of the victims? Were they chosen at random, or was there a connection Anne simply hadn't stumbled upon yet?

"All done?"

"Oh!" Anne startled, and her eyes flew open as Aurora walked into the supply room. "Sorry. I was just thinking."

"Okay. So when you're finished with the cabinet, would you mind going up to housekeeping? We're running low on socks."

She pointed to a bin half-filled with rubber-soled socks for the patients' feet.

"I can do that," Anne said, measuring her words as she set down her clipboard, "but before I do, I'd like to talk with you, if you have a minute."

Aurora Kingston was nothing if not professional. She gave a slight nod and held her hand toward the door. "Shall we step into my office?"

"Oh…all right." Leaving the supply room, Anne walked down the hall to the volunteer coordinator's office. When they got there, she opened the door and stepped back. "After you."

"Thanks." Aurora crossed to the desk, shoved a stack of folders aside, and sat. "What can I do for you, Anne?"

"Actually, I just wanted to talk to you about last week."

Aurora blinked and angled her head. "Sorry…last week?"

Surely she knew what Anne was referring to? She swallowed and started again. "When I had to be out for Addie's illness."

"Oh yes." She took out a pen and started scribbling notes across some of the folders. "I hope she's doing better now."

"She is. Thank you." She waited, but Aurora looked frazzled and distracted and said nothing further. "So, um, I've gotten the feeling that maybe you were a little disappointed that I called in last minute."

"Not at all," Aurora said quickly. Too quickly. Her voice had a sharpness to it that Anne would have been hard-pressed to miss, especially since it was so out of character for her. "Things happen," Aurora continued, lifting her gaze to meet Anne's. "I completely understand."

"Okay, well…" She hesitated. Maybe Aurora wasn't angry with her. Maybe she just needed a job done and knew she could depend on Anne to do it.

"Was there anything else?" Aurora asked, cutting into her thoughts with the tap-tapping of the pen.

Anne shook her head. "I guess not."

"Good." Aurora reached for the stack of folders and took another one off the top. "Don't forget about the socks, okay?"

"I won't." Anne stood, but Aurora was completely absorbed in the file and didn't look up. Biting back a sigh, Anne slid quietly out the door. If Aurora was upset, she'd need to figure out why some other way. In the meantime, she needed to hurry and get the socks or she'd be late for the workout.

The sock bin filled, Anne swung toward the locker room, her steps quickening. It was after five. Evelyn, Joy, and Shirley would already be waiting for her downstairs. She grabbed her tote bag out of one of the lockers and yanked the curtains closed on a changing room to slip into a comfortable set of workout clothes.

As she'd expected, her three friends were clustered around the door to the fitness studio when Anne arrived.

Evelyn tapped her watch as she approached.

"I know," Anne said, raising her hand before Evelyn could say anything. "I got busy and lost track of time. Plus, I was in Aurora's office."

"Oh?" Joy's eyes widened. "And?"

"What did she say?" Shirley chimed in, leaning forward to peer over Joy's shoulder.

"Not much. I'll tell you during class." Anne pointed inside, where Talia was already halfway through the warm-up. "Let's go."

As before, a large group had chosen to participate. The four of them grabbed mats and laid them side by side along the back row.

"Aurora said she wasn't disappointed that I was out," Anne whispered, bending over to touch her toes.

"Uh, right." Evelyn frowned and mimicked Anne's motion, but instead of actually touching her toes, braced her hands midway down her shins. "So then why has she been acting so strange?"

"No idea. She said she understands when things come up," Anne said.

Talia shifted down to the floor and the four of them followed suit.

"Maybe she just needed someone she knew she could count on," Anne said, pulling both knees in to sit cross-legged the way Talia demonstrated. "I don't know, girls. Do you think I'm just being oversensitive about this whole thing?"

"Could be." Shirley stretched one arm over her head and then the other. Finished, she shot a look sidelong at Anne. "Say, I don't think I asked you. What were you going to see Garrison about?"

Joy leaned forward to look past Shirley at Anne. "You talked to Garrison?"

"I wanted to ask him about Crystal," Anne explained, stretching out her biceps. "He said he doesn't know her all that well."

Talia stood, and from that point, the class transitioned into their cardio workout. Out of breath after just a few minutes, Anne figured she'd wait until class was over to fill her friends in on the rest. Fortunately, Talia proved to be prompt, and the class ended at exactly six, with most of the participants dispersing to head home. That gave Anne plenty of time to tell the others what she'd learned about Preston Winder and his son, which she did while Talia sanitized mats in the background.

Joy shook her head. "How sad."

"It was sad," Evelyn said. "I remember talking about it with someone. Wait—" She turned wide eyes toward Shirley. "Weren't you...?"

Shirley wiped a towel over her face then draped it over her shoulders and nodded. "I was on duty that night. It was just after I came to work at Mercy. Mr. Winder's son was in a bad accident, and we weren't able to save him. He and his wife were devastated."

"I can't even imagine." Joy raised her hand to her mouth, and she looked at Anne. "Sorry."

Anne smiled and patted her friend's shoulder. "Don't be."

Though Anne's and Ralph's hearts would forever bear the scar left by the loss of their daughter Ariane to leukemia, God had proven faithful in helping them heal and restoring their joy. "I'll have to ask Ralph if he's heard of the family."

"I doubt it." Shirley used a corner of the towel around her neck to wipe a trickle of sweat from her brow. "The hospital tried to reach out to them, but the family began litigation proceedings almost immediately after their son's passing. They just flat-out refused to believe there wasn't more we could have done." Though her voice was calm, pain pooled in the taut wrinkles around her mouth and eyes.

Anne reached for her arm and gave it a squeeze. "I'm so sorry. I know it's never easy losing a patient."

Shirley let go of the towel to pat Anne's hand. "Thanks. And you're right. I've thought about that little boy a lot."

The four of them fell silent, the only sound the swishing of a broom while Talia swept the floor. Though Anne hated to consider it, she couldn't help but wonder...

"Do you think...?"

"Maybe Preston is behind the attacks?" Evelyn finished for her. Anne nodded.

"Why would he do that if the hospital is still in litigation?" Joy asked.

"Medical malpractice suits can take years to resolve," Anne said. "Maybe he's gotten tired of waiting for the legal system to run its course."

Evelyn rubbed her hand over her chin as she chewed on the idea. "So then it's the *hospital* that connects Shirley to the other victims, not their job or a particular event."

"Not necessarily." All eyes turned to Shirley. She shrugged and repeated what she'd said. "It's not necessarily the hospital. Crystal Thompson was also on duty the night Mr. Winder's son came into the emergency room."

She couldn't have heard right. Anne frowned and shook her head. "I don't understand. Crystal works in Human Resources."

"Now, yes, but back then, she worked patient check-in. It was one of the complaints Mr. Winder had against the hospital. He felt it took too long to get the paperwork filed—time he could have spent with his son before he died."

"That's terrible. I mean the situation, not Crystal," Joy clarified.

"It really is," Anne agreed. "That's one thing I can say—Ralph and I were with Ariane when she passed. We had time to say our goodbyes."

Time, yes, but not enough. Never enough. She gave a mental shake and shifted her thoughts forward instead of back. One day they'd see their daughter again, and then time wouldn't matter.

Anne drew in a deep, steadying breath. "All right then, for the moment, let's assume there is a connection. How do we go about finding out more about Preston Winder?"

"I can do some checking," Evelyn volunteered quickly. "I'm sure there will be plenty of information about him online."

Joy moved to Evelyn's side. "I'll help."

Anne nodded at them both. "Good. We'll talk more tomorrow."

They said their goodbyes, and then Evelyn strolled with Joy out of the fitness studio. Anne envied Joy's loose walk. She seemed unfazed by the workout, while Anne felt the ache in every muscle.

"How does she do it?" Shirley broke into her thoughts and pointed toward Joy. "Even my fingernails are sore, and she looks like she just stepped out of a spa."

Anne started to stretch one arm, winced, and stopped. "I was thinking the exact same thing. I'll be lucky if I can crawl out of bed tomorrow. It's not the cardio that's getting me." She gently prodded the muscles of her thighs. "It's all the stretching beforehand."

"Exactly. Who knew Joy was so bendy?"

Catching sight of the woman who'd been talking with Julie earlier, Anne straightened and angled her head in her direction. "Speaking of being sore, do you know Marilyn Dodson?"

Shirley followed her gaze across the studio. "I've run into her a couple of times in the cafeteria. She seems nice. Why?"

"I overheard her talking with Julie today. It sounded like maybe she'd been passed up for a promotion. Do you know who she works for?"

Shirley thought a moment then shook her head. "I don't, but it wouldn't be hard to find out." She angled her chin at Anne curiously. "Any particular reason why you're interested?"

Anne lifted one shoulder in a shrug. "Oh, you know...disgruntled employee, passed over one too many times for someone younger with less experience. It's a familiar story, and one I'm thinking could be tied to possible motive. Anyway, it's just a hunch." Anne pushed her sleeve up to glance at her watch. It was quarter past six. Lili would have picked up Addie by now, but Anne still had fifteen minutes before Ralph had suggested they meet up for dinner. She looked at Shirley hopefully. "I'm going to grab something to drink. Wanna come with me?"

Shirley also glanced at her watch. "Sounds good, but I may have to take mine with me so Mama's not waiting. She watches the clock like a hawk nowadays, and if I'm a minute later than I said I'd be, she calls to ask where I am."

Anne agreed, and the two of them walked out through the lobby to the coffee shop. Even at this time of the evening, the scent of freshly ground beans lingered on the air. While they waited for their order to be prepared, Anne asked about Preston.

"So tell me about that night," she said, just loudly enough to be heard over the whir of the blender. "What happened?"

Shirley backed up a step to rest her shoulder against the wall, and her gaze grew distant. "It was pretty awful. One of the parents pulled out of the driveway and didn't see him playing behind the car until it was too late."

Anne's chest tightened. An accident like this was every parent's nightmare. "*One* of the parents?"

"I never was clear on which one was driving," Shirley said. "They were in such a panic, they didn't call 911 or wait for an ambulance. They just scooped the boy up and drove him straight to the emergency room."

Anne pressed her hand to her heart. "Oh, Shirley."

"Uh-huh. My heart broke for them." She paused, her dark eyes troubled. "Honestly, when all this first happened, I didn't want to believe there was any sort of connection between me and the other victims. Now, with Crystal also being on duty, I'm not so sure."

"We could be wrong about Preston," Anne said, lowering her voice so as not to be overheard. Now that the blender was off, the shop felt too quiet, and there were several customers lingering at tables.

"Maybe." She started to say more, then stopped and shook her head. That made two times Anne thought there was something bothering Shirley that she couldn't quite bring herself to say.

"What's the matter?" Anne asked.

Shirley sighed and shoved upright off the wall. "It's going to sound strange, I know…" She looked at Anne, her mouth working as she released another sigh. "The person who hit me—I don't think they meant to hurt me."

Anne's mouth fell open. "What?"

"Green tea for Anne! Iced coffee for Shirley."

Anne turned toward the counter as her name was called. "Stay here, Shirley. I'll be right back."

Anne grabbed the drinks then rejoined Shirley near the wall. "Okay, what were you saying about the attacker? What do you mean, they didn't want to hurt you?"

She handed the cup to Shirley, but neither of them took a drink. Shirley's lid groaned as she drew the straw up and down.

"I mean, they came up from behind me and all that, but after I fell, they didn't leave right away. They stood there a second, like they wanted to make sure I was okay before they ran off."

"Shirley..."

"Trust me, I know. I said it would sound strange." She lifted her hand to rub thoughtfully at her temple. "It's just a feeling, I guess. I can't really explain it."

Anne fell silent a moment and then said, "Did you mention this to the police?"

Shirley dropped her hand and shook her head. "I didn't think about it when I was giving my statement. It was only later, when I'd had time to reflect, that I remembered lying on the ground and seeing their shoes."

Anne startled at the words. "You saw their shoes? What kind were they?" When Shirley didn't answer right away, Anne clasped her arm. "Shirley, their shoes. What kind were they? Do you know?"

She blinked and then stammered, "Wh-white. Like—"

"Nurses' shoes." Which made perfect sense, considering both attacks had taken place at the hospital.

"Um..."

Or they could have been athletic shoes, like a few of the other staff wore. Anne's thoughts sped in a blinding whirl. Like the kind Marilyn had been wearing when she saw her earlier that day.

Marilyn—who'd been so angry at being passed over for a promotion that she'd knocked the clipboard from Julie's hand. What had she been about to say before being interrupted by Anne's presence? And perhaps a better question...

Where was she the night Shirley was attacked?

Chapter Seven

WHILE AURORA HADN'T APPEARED TO warm up any overnight, she did put Anne back on other duties, something she was grateful for as she assisted an elderly couple with their discharge on Thursday. Inventory was a necessary job, but Anne much preferred helping people.

"Are you sure we got everything out of the room, Doris?" The man peered up from his wheelchair at the silver-haired woman at his elbow. Both were dressed neatly in slacks and matching sweaters, but hers was adorned with a silver pin fastened at the shoulder that glinted when she moved.

"That's the third time you've asked, George," she grumbled as they crossed the lobby toward the exit.

Anne slowed the wheelchair to peer over George's shoulder into his face, giving her a whiff of the cologne he'd applied liberally before leaving the room. "I could go back up and do one final check for you, if you'd like."

His pale eyes lit hopefully. "Would you mind? I'd just hate to leave anything behind and have to come back for it later."

"Oh, George." Doris patted his arm impatiently. "Don't make the poor woman go back upstairs."

"It's no trouble at all," Anne assured them. "I'll be back before you know it."

She left them near the entrance then hurried upstairs to their room. As she suspected, a quick sweep of the bathroom and closet revealed nothing. Still, it made her feel good to see George relax a bit as she returned empty-handed to help him into the car.

"Take care of yourself," she said then shut the car door and sent them off with a wave.

Outside, falling temperatures had turned the October air crisp. Even in Charleston, autumn color tinged the treetops, but Anne didn't linger to admire their beauty. Rubbing her arms, she hurried inside where it was warmer.

"Hey, you." Joy waved to her from the gift shop. "Did Aurora let you out of inventory?"

"Looks like it." Anne motioned to the rear counter. "Got any coffee on?"

"Always." Joy looped her arm through Anne's and walked with her to the back of the store. "I'm glad I caught you. Have you talked to Evelyn?"

"Not yet." Anne straightened hopefully. "Did you find out something about Preston?"

"The opposite, I'm afraid." Joy handed her a cup of coffee then crossed her arms and leaned against the counter. "Evelyn's computer has been acting up. This morning it crashed completely. She was going to call you to see if you wanted to head downtown to the Charleston Library today to do some digging."

Anne took mental inventory of her schedule then nodded. "I can do that. I'll text her and let her know. I only have one more patient to walk down after lunch, and then it's just checking in with the other departments to see if they need anything."

"Great. Keep me updated, okay?"

"Will do."

"Creamer is in the fridge," Joy said, pointing.

"Hold up." Anne snagged her arm and then tossed a quick glance around the gift shop. Except for a young mom and her daughter looking through *Get Well* cards, they were alone. She turned back to Joy. "Have you got a sec?"

"Sure." Joy lowered her voice to match Anne's. "What's going on?"

"It's about last night, after you and Evelyn left from working out." Anne filled her in on what Shirley had said and about the possible connection to Marilyn.

Joy's eyes widened as she listened. "That's interesting." She blinked and snapped her gaze to Anne's. "Has she told the police?"

"She's doing that today. It might not help at all, but still…"

"Right." Joy pinched her lip and frowned. "So now we have two suspects to worry about."

"Looks like it." Anne took a sip of her coffee, puckered at the bitter taste, then opened the fridge and took out the creamer. "Anyway, I wanted you to know what was going on. And I'll fill Evelyn in when I see her this afternoon."

"Okay."

The young woman had moved to the cash register.

"Gotta go," Joy said, spotting her.

Anne nodded, added a generous bit of creamer to her coffee, snapped on a lid, and left the store. After sending a brief text to Evelyn about a meeting time, she wove through the hospital toward the chapel and Ralph's office. He sat at his desk, a notebook he used to keep track of his appointments open in front of him, and his chin resting on his steepled fingers.

Immediately, his eyes brightened when he saw her. "Hey, sweetheart. This is a nice surprise." He shut the notebook then got up and rounded the desk to press a light kiss to her temple. "What are you up to?"

"I just wanted to pop in and let you know I was heading downtown with Evelyn in about an hour."

"Downtown?" His eyebrows rose. "Is this about Shirley?"

Her husband always could read her like a book. Anne smiled and set her coffee on the edge of his desk.

Giving a grunt, Ralph pulled out a chair and joined her. "Okay. What's going on?"

Anne filled him in on their theories, then took a sip from her cup. "Anyway, we're going to the library to see what we can find out about Preston."

Ralph gestured toward his desk. "Do you want to use my computer? I hate for you to have to drive downtown during rush hour."

Anne thought a moment and then shook her head. "I have no idea how long we'll be, and I don't want to tie up your computer." She motioned to him. "What were you doing? You looked pretty deep in thought when I came in."

"That's because I was." He reached across his desk for his phone and slid it to her. "Take a look at Lili's text. The school nurse called. Addie went home sick again today. I was just looking through my appointments to see if I could shift things around so I can sit with her tomorrow."

"What?" Anne grabbed his phone and scrolled down to Lili's message. "Why didn't she text me?"

"Probably because she didn't want you to miss another day of work and get into trouble like last time," Ralph said.

Anne snorted and shoved the phone back at him. "I'm a volunteer, Ralph."

"Tell that to Aurora," he replied gently. "Especially right now."

"What are you talking about?"

His gaze fell, and he leaned back in his chair to fold his hands across his midriff.

"Ralph?" Anne angled her head at him curiously. "Has Aurora been to see you?"

"In an official capacity only," he said.

She knew what that meant without needing more explanation. As chaplain of the hospital, he wouldn't be able to share what they'd talked about. Anne pressed her lips together firmly. So she was right. There was more going on with Aurora than she'd let on.

Anne patted his knee and stood. "I'll be praying for you, honey. And Aurora too."

"Thanks, sweetheart." He rose too and kissed her goodbye. "Are you working out tonight?"

"Nope. But I think Evelyn and I are going to get some dinner after we leave the library. Would you like me to bring you something?"

"Don't bother. I can grab a burger on my way home."

"It's no bother. I'll pick something up."

"Okay." He gave her another quick kiss then reached for her coffee cup. "Don't forget this."

"You drink it," Anne said, laying her hand against the tired lines on his cheek. "You look like you need it more than I do."

She moved toward the door, looking back just in time to see Ralph take a sip from her cup, grimace, and set it aside. Chuckling, Anne shut the door. Apparently, pumpkin spice wasn't his thing.

The rest of the afternoon passed quickly, with Anne checking her watch often until it was time to meet Evelyn outside the records department. She was just locking up as Anne arrived, her laptop clutched under one arm and the cord dangling at her feet.

"Here, let me help before you trip," Anne said, reaching for the cord. "What's going on with your computer?"

"Beats me." Evelyn huffed and shifted the laptop to her other arm. "Mind if I drop this off with IT before we go?"

"Not at all."

They made the quick detour and then Evelyn drove them along East Bay Street toward Calhoun, where the library was located. Constructed of red brick with an off-white façade decorating the entrance, it was an imposing building, and one of only two libraries in South Carolina to survive the Civil War. The city was proud of this fact, and special care had been taken to adorn the building with pumpkins and mums for fall.

"Here we are." Evelyn pulled into a parking spot then reached into the back seat for her purse. "Let's get to work."

Inside, bluish-green carpeting and shelves stuffed with books muffled their steps as they wound toward a row of computers near a large bank of windows that overlooked the lawn. When she spied an unused one, Anne hurried over to it and pulled out the chair for Evelyn.

"You do the typing. You're faster than I am."

Evelyn agreed and stowed her things under her chair while the computer came out of hibernation. "First things first."

She bit her lip and typed Preston Winder's name into the search bar. A list of businesses, people, and equipment filled the screen. Realizing the wording was too broad, Evelyn narrowed their search to South Carolina, and then Charleston.

"There's something," Anne said, pointing, but then pulled her finger away when she realized what they were reading was the obituary for Preston's son.

"Oh dear. That's so sad," Evelyn said, when she finished.

"It gets worse." Anne shared what Shirley had told her, then sat back in her chair. "I don't know, Evelyn. I just don't feel right about looking into this family. They've been through so much."

And it hits too close to home.

Evelyn hesitated. "But you said it yourself. The legal system can be slow. Maybe he just got tired of waiting."

Anne swallowed hard as a wash of emotions she'd thought long buried flooded over her. Sorrow. Discouragement. Fear. They were a bitter potion that reappeared when Anne was least ready for them.

Across from them, a student wearing a marine biology sweatshirt from the College of Charleston shut off her computer and gathered up her things.

Evelyn seemed to sense what she was feeling and patted her arm. "Hey, why don't you go over there and see what you can find out about the other attacks? I'll take care of the Winders."

Nodding in relief, Anne grabbed her purse and circled around to the empty computer station. Like Evelyn, Anne needed a few minutes to narrow her search enough to pull only attacks that had taken place at or near the hospital and only in recent weeks. Anne read through a couple of articles, then paused her scrolling when she stumbled on a third that detailed an attack at a restaurant not far from the hospital.

"Hey, Evelyn?"

Evelyn's head popped up over her computer monitor, the glow from the screen making her face pale. "Yeah?"

"Do you remember that new guy…the janitor at the hospital who made Talia so nervous?"

"Benny Pierce?"

Anne nodded.

"What about him?"

She beckoned, and Evelyn rose to come and stand next to her. On Anne's screen was a grainy picture of Benny.

"Hey, look at that." Evelyn leaned forward to squint at the monitor. "What does the caption say?"

"It's an older article." Anne pointed at the date in the header. "From last year. But it looks like he was arrested for brawling at a restaurant close to the hospital."

Evelyn frowned. "What? How did you find that?"

"I typed in *attack* and *hospital* and this was one of the links that popped up."

Evelyn nudged Anne in the ribs. "Move over. Let me see what it says."

Anne slid out of the chair and Evelyn sat in silence, her lips moving while she read. The article wasn't exactly about Benny. Instead, the focus was more on the rising number of disputes outside of local pubs and what could be done to prevent them. Evelyn pointed to the name of the restaurant where the incident involving Benny had taken place.

"That's not far from here, and we said we'd get a bite to eat when we finished. Want to check it out?"

"Couldn't hurt." Anne angled her head toward Evelyn's computer. "Are you done for the night?"

"I think so. I found some stuff, but nothing we didn't already know." Evelyn circled back around, shut down the computer, and then scooped up her purse and keys. "Let's go."

It was early yet, only a few minutes after six. Still, a large number of people clustered near the entrance to McLarty's Food and Beverage waiting for a table. Anne gave her name to the hostess then joined Evelyn at the door. "Busy place."

"Uh-huh. The food must be good." She tipped her head back and sniffed, then nodded toward the bar, where several men gathered around television screens hung high on the walls. "Either that or it's a popular place to watch the game."

"Table for two, ladies?" A waiter in a black shirt and jeans took two menus from the hostess stand and looked questioningly at Anne.

She nodded.

"Follow me," he said.

Thankfully, he led them to a table far away from the noise of the bar. Anne ordered a Coke and Evelyn asked for tea before they both slipped into the booth and flipped open their menus.

"So?" Evelyn shot a narrowed glance around the restaurant. "What's the plan? How do we go about asking what happened with Benny?"

Anne frowned, thinking. "We could check with the waiter. Maybe he knows something."

Evelyn agreed. After several minutes, the waiter returned with their drinks.

"Sorry about the wait." He set the frosted glasses down with a *thunk*. "The football game is on tonight, and the boys get here early."

"No problem." Anne curled her fingers around the chilled glass and slid it closer.

The waiter pulled a notepad from a pocket of his apron. "Y'all ready to order?"

Anne looked at Evelyn for approval, who nodded.

"How's the corned beef?" Anne asked.

"Reuben on rye is one of our customer favorites," he replied, flipping the pages on his notepad.

Anne nodded. "I'll take that. And can you add a side of onion rings?"

Evelyn folded her menu and laid it aside. "Make that two."

"Will do." He scribbled fast and then shoved the notepad back into his pocket.

The waiter looked harried, so rather than pepper him with questions, Anne let him go. "Maybe things will slow down in a bit," she said.

In fact, the opposite was true. By the time their food arrived, there was not a single open table in the place, and the crowd around the bar had swelled to twice its size.

Anne picked up her glass and rattled the ice cubes in the bottom. "Ugh. Do you see our waiter anywhere?"

Evelyn drained the last bit of tea from her own glass and frowned. "Nope. But maybe—"

"Sorry, ladies. Can I get you more to drink?" A handsome-looking man in his late thirties or forties, bald-headed and with a graying beard, ducked into view. The name of the restaurant was printed on his shirt, but instead of an apron, he wore a gray vest and black slacks. A black leather bracelet circled his wrist, and tattoos covered both arms.

"Um…" Anne scanned the restaurant. "We were just looking for our waiter."

"I'm Max McLarty, the owner." He held out his hand to each of them in turn. "Have I seen you in here before?"

"First time," Evelyn said.

"Well, we're glad to have you." He looked at the mostly eaten sandwich on Anne's plate. "How was the Reuben?"

"Delicious. I just couldn't eat it all."

"Glad to hear it." He held out his hand toward their glasses. "Now, how 'bout those drinks?"

"Coke for me," Anne said.

"And I had sweet tea."

"Coming right up." Max melted into the crowd and reappeared a few minutes later with their drinks in one hand. In the other, he balanced two slices of apple pie with scoops of vanilla ice cream melting over the sides. Setting them down with a flourish, he said, "There's always room for dessert, right? On the house."

"Oh, you didn't need to do that," Anne protested.

"First timers always get special treatment." He rested one hand on the back of an unused chair and smiled. "So what brings you ladies in? How did you hear about us?"

Spying the perfect opening, Anne leaned forward. "Actually, we read about you in the paper."

Max's chest puffed slightly, stretching the buttons on his vest, and his smile broadened. "Did the Reader's Choice list come out already? I thought that wasn't going to print until next week."

Anne licked her lips nervously. "Um, Reader's Choice?"

"That's where newspaper subscribers vote on their favorite local businesses," Evelyn said.

"McLarty's was voted Best Casual Dining," Max added, the pride in his voice obvious.

Anne smiled. "Congratulations."

"Thanks."

"But that's not how we heard about you," she continued.

"No?" He scratched his beard.

"It was actually another article. One that came out last year, about a brawl that took place here involving a guy named Benny Pierce."

The confusion cleared from Max's face, replaced by a dark scowl. "Oh, that. Yeah, that guy is a real piece of work. Always looking for trouble. He came in here quite a bit before the fight. I had to ban him permanently afterward, so I haven't seen him since."

Evelyn sat forward. "When you say he looked for trouble, what do you mean?"

"Oh, you know, the usual stuff. Benny has a quick temper, never backs away when something hits him crossways."

Anne matched Evelyn's posture and rested her elbows on the table. "That night in particular, do you remember what the argument was about?"

"Ping-pong." Max grunted and pulled a ladder-back chair away from the table next to them. After spinning it around, he sat, his arms resting on the top rung. "There was nothing on TV that night, just some reruns of a ping-pong match from the last Olympics. If you can believe it, old Benny got to jawing with another customer and it led to a fight. Three tables and a mess of busted dishes later, I had to throw them both out. Benny was the one hurt most from it though."

"What do you mean?" Evelyn asked.

Max shrugged and pushed up from the chair. "My place was one of the few that still allowed him in. If he's not careful, there won't be a restaurant or bar in Charleston that'll allow him within fifty feet." He tipped his head to each of them before turning to go. "Enjoy the pie, ladies."

"What do you make of that?" Evelyn asked, reaching for her fork as Max left.

"Sounds like Benny Pierce has quite a temper." Anne grabbed her own fork and sliced off a bite of pie. "Mmm, it's still warm."

"Mmm is right." Evelyn tapped her fork against the rim of her plate. "I'd have to take a whole lot more of Talia's classes if I ate this every day."

"But it's totally worth it today." Anne speared a slice of apple dripping with cinnamon and sugar and popped it into her mouth. "Going back to Benny," she said, after swallowing her bite, "I didn't see anything else written about him in the papers, did you?"

"No. Of course, we weren't really looking," Evelyn said, wiping her chin with a napkin.

Remembering the way Benny had watched them after Talia's class, Anne paused. "Maybe we should."

"Should what?" Evelyn licked a bit of syrup off her finger then reached for a second napkin.

"Look into Benny. I remember thinking I wanted to find out more about him, but then the thing with Preston came up and I forgot."

Evelyn shrugged. "Want me to see what I can find out? I'll have time tomorrow, especially if my computer is still acting up."

"Would you mind?"

"Not at all, but tonight…" Evelyn broke off a buttery bite of crust and held it at eye level. "Tonight, I'm going to enjoy every bit of this pie."

After breaking off her own piece of crust, Anne touched it lightly to Evelyn's. "Here's to pie."

They laughed and for the first time all day, Anne felt herself relax. Tonight, they'd eat pie and worry about resuming their investigation tomorrow. Because, like Scarlett O'Hara, Anne was sure things would be better in the morning.

They almost had to be.

Chapter Eight

ANNE FIDDLED WITH THE COVER on her cell phone, caught between her duty to the hospital and a desire to check on her granddaughter.

"Morning, sweetheart." Ralph ambled into the kitchen, his hair still damp and smelling like shampoo from his shower, and pressed a kiss to Anne's cheek before reaching for a coffee cup. "Were you on a call?" He nodded to the cell phone in her hand.

Anne set it down with a sigh. "Yeah. I just got done talking to Lili about Addie."

"And? How's she doing? She feeling any better this morning?" He poured a cup then replaced the pot on the warmer.

"Not really. She ran a low-grade fever last night. I'm thinking about going over there."

She glanced sidelong at her husband for his reaction. Ralph just nodded, pulled the toaster out from one of the cupboards, set it on the counter, and plugged it in.

"Want some breakfast?"

"No, thanks." She pushed away from the sink and crossed her arms. "Aren't you going to say something?"

Leaving the toaster, he walked to her and rubbed both her arms gently. This close, she could smell the scent of pine soap lingering on his skin and see the small bit of shaving cream he'd missed clinging to his ear. "Would it make you feel better if you saw Addie?"

She flicked the shaving cream away with her thumb. "Of course it would."

"Then go."

She peered into his eyes and saw love and warmth. He wasn't teasing, and his tone wasn't condescending. She relaxed a little. "Do you think I should?"

He grabbed his cup and brought it to his mouth to hide a small smile. "Now that is an entirely different question."

"Ralph." She smacked his shoulder playfully.

"Okay." He set down his coffee and looked her fully in the eyes. "I understand being worried, but it's probably just a bug, sweetheart. Addie's only missed one day of school."

"Two, counting last week."

"Fine, two. But it's October. Kids get sick."

"I know but—"

"Did Lili ask you to come over?"

She gritted her teeth, her hackles rising defensively. "No."

"So how do you think she'll feel if you go rushing over there anyway? Do you think it might be better if you just stopped by on your way home from work?"

He was right, much as she hated to admit it. She spun and grabbed a loaf of bread from out of the breadbox. "How many slices do you want?"

"Two, please."

He didn't smirk. Smart man. She grinned at him and plunked two slices of bread into the toaster then jammed the lever down. "What do you have planned today?"

"Patient visits, mostly, plus a couple of stops before I make rounds."

"Speaking of patients…" Anne filled him in on the Winder family and also what she'd learned about Benny last night. "We can't cross Marilyn Dodson off our list either," she said, pulling the butter and grape jelly out of the fridge just as the toast popped up. "She's a disgruntled employee, though it would be quite a leap for her to go from merely being upset to violent."

Except—

She thought back on what Shirley had said about her attacker not wanting to hurt her. Could that be why? But then why target Shirley? Or Crystal?

She froze. Marilyn had said she'd been passed up *again*. Had she applied for Crystal's job? That might explain why she'd chosen to target her, but what about Shirley or the other two victims?

And these were only the disgruntled employees that she knew about.

"Hey." Ralph snapped his fingers in front of Anne's face. "There you are," he said as she turned her focus to him.

"Sorry, what did you say?"

He laughed and took the butter and jelly out of her hands. "I said the toast is getting cold."

She laughed too. "Sorry."

He quirked an eyebrow and took a knife out of the drawer. "Want me to fix you a slice?"

"No, thanks. I'll pick up a smoothie on my way to the hospital. Bye, sweetheart. Oh, and you're right about Addie. I'm meeting up with the girls this afternoon, but I'll swing by after our workout."

She gave him a kiss then grabbed her coat and purse and headed to the car. Outside, a cold drizzle had begun to fall, which made navigating the streets slower. Anne flipped her hood up over her head before hurrying inside the hospital to the volunteer office, where Aurora was posting the day's schedule. Today, her bun looked especially messy, with dark curls spilling out over her shoulders.

"Morning, Aurora."

"Morning." She sniffled but didn't look at Anne, just continued pushing pins into the board. "Please make sure you look at the schedule before you start for the day. Lots of changes."

"Okay. Thanks."

Aurora didn't answer, just disappeared into her office and shut the door.

She's upset about something, and this time it's not me.

Anne shrugged out of her sweater and headed to the locker room to grab her smock. She and Aurora weren't close, their relationship mostly on a professional level. But she was hurting. And while Anne didn't know what was wrong, God did. She could pray for her.

Thankful the locker room was empty, Anne spent a quiet moment praying for Aurora. When she was done, she pulled on a clean smock and fastened her name tag to it. That finished, she checked the schedule before heading toward discharge for her first patient of the day. Barely had she reached the nurses' station when her cell pinged in her pocket.

A text. She didn't look at it. Phones were discouraged when volunteers were on duty. A second ping followed the first, then another. And another. All in rapid succession.

Was it the school? Could it be about Addie?

Anne's heart thumped. Instead of approaching the nurses' station, she swung toward an empty hall and yanked her phone out to look. The messages weren't from the school. They were from Evelyn. And Joy. And Shirley. Several from Shirley.

Swiping her finger across the screen, Anne started at the top and scrolled quickly through the texts, but it was the last one that made her blood run cold. This one was from Evelyn, and it read simply...

THERE'S BEEN ANOTHER ATTACK.

Chapter Nine

ANNE TAPPED OUT A BRIEF response on her phone. WHAT HAPPENED?

Evelyn responded first. NO IDEA. CAN YOU MEET?

NOT UNTIL AFTER LUNCH, Anne typed back.

A message from Joy popped onto the screen. ME NEITHER. NO ONE TO WATCH THE STORE TODAY.

There was a pause, and then Evelyn replied, WHAT ABOUT AFTER WORK? WE CAN MEET OUTSIDE THE STUDIO BEFORE WE WORK OUT.

THAT'S GOOD FOR ME. The message was from Shirley. Anne agreed, and a second later, so did Joy.

Sighing, Anne replaced her phone in her pocket and continued to the nurses' station for her first discharge patient. The nurses were talking when Anne approached. By the way they whispered, she got the feeling it was about the same topic she and the girls had been discussing.

They stopped when she stepped up to the desk. "I'm here for Layla Washington."

"Room 214," the nurse at the computer said, angling her head down the hall to her left.

"Thanks." While Anne wanted to ask questions, it wasn't fair to the patient, who was probably waiting to be taken downstairs. Anne veered away from the nurses' station, found the correct room number, and then helped the patient collect her things before settling her in a wheelchair and walking her down to the lobby. The rest of the day passed quietly, with Anne catching snippets of conversation here and there. Always, the theme was this latest attack. By the time she joined Evelyn, Joy, and Shirley outside the fitness studio, she'd pieced together a fuzzy picture of what had happened.

"So did you hear? It was another nurse." Evelyn had already changed into a pair of yoga pants and a loose-fitting T-shirt. She slid her arms through the straps on her backpack and hitched them onto her shoulders. "A woman."

All around them, the buzz among the people gathered for class was the same—talk of attackers and self-defense classes instead of cardio.

Shirley raised one hand in the air. "I haven't heard. I've been home with Mama."

"Apparently, it took place a little after eight, just like the others," Joy said, fidgeting with a piece of hair that flopped over one eye.

"It was south of the Grove this time," Evelyn added.

"Do we know who the victim was?" Shirley asked. "And whether or not she was hurt?"

"Her name is Susan Merchant," Anne said. "Apparently her attacker came up from behind, just like with you."

Shirley jerked her head up quickly. "I know Susan. She's a surgical nurse." She looked at Anne, and her voice trembled with excitement. "She's only been with the hospital about six months."

Anne was quick to catch on to her meaning. "So, she couldn't have been on duty the night Preston's son died."

"No. Maybe we were wrong about him."

She sounded as relieved as Anne felt. "I have to say, I wouldn't be upset if we were."

"Except where does that leave us?" Joy asked. "We're no closer to figuring out who the culprit is than when we started."

"I might have a couple of ideas." Anne gestured toward the back of the studio. "Let's get changed, and I'll tell you what I'm thinking."

Inside the changing room, each of them slid into a different stall, except for Evelyn, who kept an eye out for anyone who might come in. Unlike the tile in the studio, here gray carpet covered the floor, and while it looked clean, Anne could imagine the hundreds of sweaty feet that had trodden over it. She set her bag on a bench, kicked off her shoes, and spoke quietly through the curtain. "So Evelyn and I stumbled across a bit of information about Benny Pierce."

She told them what Max McLarty had said and then what she'd learned about Marilyn Dodson.

"The problem with Marilyn is, I can't figure out why she would want to target Shirley."

"Hold on." The curtain on Shirley's stall scraped back, and then Anne saw her feet outside her own stall. "You said she just recently got passed over for a promotion?"

"Uh-huh." Anne tugged a T-Shirt over her head, then pulled a ponytail holder out of her bag and stepped out from behind her curtain. "Hey, did you have a chance to ask who her boss is?"

"Didn't I tell you?" Shirley frowned and rubbed her fingers over her head. "That bump I took must be worse than I thought. She's Marcus Seybold's administrative assistant."

"Huh."

Behind them, the changing room door swung open and Julie entered, talking to Talia over her shoulder. Though Anne couldn't hear all that was said, she did make out Preston Winder's name. Was Julie telling her what had happened with his son?

Soon, their voices faded and a wall of lockers blocked them from sight.

"You girls ready?" Joy pulled her curtain back. Dressed in close-fitting gray pants and a matching tank, she appeared fit and trim and full of energy.

Anne eyed her from head to toe. "Wow. You look great."

Joy ran her hands down her sides. "Really?"

"You seem full of energy," Shirley agreed. "These classes must be working."

Joy looked quite pleased as she led the way out of the changing room. Pausing at the door, Anne looked back for Julie and Talia. Julie had disappeared, but Talia stood in front of a locker, carefully removing a necklace from around her neck. She laid it inside then rested her hand on top. When she turned and saw Anne holding the door, she shut the locker with a bang and hurried over.

"Thanks."

"No problem." Anne angled her head toward the locker. "Is that the seahorse necklace?"

Talia's brown eyes widened in surprise.

"I noticed you wearing it the first night of class," Anne explained. "It's really beautiful."

She flashed a bright smile. "Thanks. I got it on vacation in the Bahamas, but the clasp is loose and I don't want to risk losing it."

"The Bahamas, huh? I've always wanted to go."

"Oh, you definitely should. I went in July." Talia's smile dimmed slightly. "It was the trip of a lifetime."

Why would that fact make her sad?

"Maybe you can go back sometime," Anne said.

"Maybe." Talia fidgeted with her ponytail, never quite meeting Anne's eyes, then cleared her throat. "We should probably get started," she continued, feet shuffling.

"Of course." Anne held the door wider and followed Talia into the studio. Evelyn had already grabbed an extra mat and waved Anne over.

"Everything okay?"

"Fine," Anne said, unrolling the mat with a flick of her wrists. But she watched Talia with new eyes during class. Dressed in a black and red long-sleeved fitness suit, with Crossfit gloves and athletic shoes, she seemed outwardly strong and confident. Exuberant. Polished, even. But something in the way Talia responded when speaking about her trip to the Bahamas made Anne wonder if, deep down, Talia suffered from some type of insecurity.

Julie popped out of the changing room and took her place on the end of one of the rows. Marilyn was missing, Anne noted, not that her presence, or lack of, was significant. She'd been at the last class, but maybe she'd tried it and decided cardio workouts weren't for her.

On and on Anne's thoughts circled, until finally, she threw herself into the workout, legs pumping until sweat trickled from her brow. It felt good. Like she'd accomplished something. Which was nice. Because solving this mystery? Well, she hadn't accomplished anything.

And at the moment, she wasn't sure she ever would.

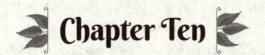

Chapter Ten

ANNE'S INTERNAL ALARM CLOCK WENT off early Saturday morning, long before the chickadees started singing. She buried her head under her pillow with a sigh. Hard as she tried, it had proven impossible over the years to convince her body that weekends were meant for sleeping in. Ralph, however, sawed logs next to her.

Nothing for it then. She might as well get up.

Pushing her feet into a pair of fuzzy slippers, Anne yawned, stretched, and then padded to the kitchen to start the coffee brewing. Soon the warm, toasty aroma tickled her senses, drawing her to even greater wakefulness.

Anne pulled a chair to the kitchen window, sipping her coffee as she sat looking out. Mornings in Charleston were dazzling, with the dew on the grass sparkling like jewels and a fine mist rising from the streets to cloak the earth in ghostly white.

Muffled buzzing disrupted her quiet contemplation. It was her phone, and it was coming from her purse. She must have forgotten to plug it in after she got home from visiting with Lili and Addie.

She scrambled to get to it before the call disconnected. Seeing it was Shirley who called, she punched the answer button and pressed the phone to her ear. "You're up early."

"So are you. Did I wake you?"

"Nope. I'm halfway through my first cup of coffee." She returned to the table to sit. "What's going on?"

"I couldn't sleep. I kept replaying the attack in my head and thinking about Susan. I almost called her."

"You should. Maybe it would help you both to talk."

"Maybe." The line crackled a bit, and then Shirley returned. "Did you tell Ralph about this latest victim?"

"He already knew. The hospital asked him to meet with Susan and her family after she got done talking with police."

"And?"

"Nothing. Susan never saw her attacker, and the police weren't able to capture any footage."

Shirley's exasperated sigh echoed how Anne had felt when she first heard the news.

"Well, that's too bad. I really was hoping this time they'd have a strong lead," Shirley said.

"Me too." Anne fingered the ruffled edge of one of the place-mats on the table. "I'm really sorry, Shirl."

"What on earth do you have to be sorry for?"

"I really hoped by now we'd have stumbled onto something that would help."

"You're doing everything you can. So am I, and so are Evelyn and Joy. Don't you let yourself get discouraged."

Though Shirley couldn't see it, Anne smiled.

"I did think of something I wanted to run by you," Shirley continued. "I told you Susan wasn't on duty the night Preston's son died?"

"Yes, I remember."

"Well, she was assisting during another surgery where the patient died. I remember her talking about it right after it happened. She took it hard. It was her first time losing a patient."

Anne tightened her grip on the phone. "Shirley, do you think that means Preston...I mean...whoever is behind the attacks," she corrected, "might be expanding their targets?"

"I wondered the same thing. That's why I called you."

Anne glanced at the clock on the stove. "We should call Evelyn and Joy and talk about it. Are you free for lunch?"

"I can be," Shirley said. "Where do you want to meet?"

"Let's come here. Talking about it at your house would be too upsetting for your mom."

"Okay. You call Joy. I'll get ahold of Evelyn."

They agreed on a time and hung up. Anne made breakfast, a pan of scrambled eggs and toast, then went upstairs to wake Ralph before she showered and changed. To her surprise, he was already up and mostly dressed except for his shoes.

Anne grabbed them from behind the door and handed them to him. "Where are you off to so early?"

"Sorry, sweetheart." Ralph perched on the edge of the bed to tie his shoes. "The hospital called. They need me to counsel one of the patients."

Though it was one of his more difficult roles, it was one Ralph took very seriously. He grabbed a jacket from the bedpost where he'd hung it and shoved his arms into the sleeves. "I'll be back sometime after lunch."

"No rush. The girls are coming over so we can talk."

"Okay. Love you." He gave her a kiss then strode out the door, his attention already focused on the people he would meet and what he would say to them.

"Lord, give him the words to speak comfort to this family," Anne whispered, watching him go. For what was surely the hundredth time, she marveled at how strong her husband was to be able to bear the burdens of complete strangers with such compassion. God had certainly gifted Ralph with some broad shoulders, but He'd also made him wise enough to know where to go when it was time to refresh his spirit.

Humming to herself, she washed and dressed then went back to the kitchen to prepare a chicken salad for lunch. Fortunately, she had half a loaf of French bread left from her last trip to the grocery store, and it still smelled fresh. She sliced it up and laid it out on a plate before adding a few slices of Muenster cheese, some pickles and tomatoes, and an array of nuts for anyone who wanted some crunch in their chicken salad. That done, she put some water on to boil for tea. The doorbell rang just as the kettle began whistling.

Anne poked her head into the hall and spotted Shirley through the glass on the front door. "Come on in," she called then went to the cupboard to fetch her favorite crystal pitcher for the tea.

Shirley strolled into the kitchen carrying a platter of brownies. Anne's mouth watered at the sight of them. "Are those...?"

Shirley nodded and lifted one corner of the plastic wrap, releasing a cozy, chocolate-scented cloud. "Mama sent them. She stayed up late baking last night, but this morning she didn't want them in the house. Said she'd gained five pounds just smelling them." She laughed and set the platter on the counter. "What can I do?"

"You want to set the table?" Anne motioned toward the cupboard above the sink. "Plates and cups are there, silverware is in the top drawer."

"Got it." Shirley swung the cupboard door open, took out four plates, and held up a fifth. "Is Ralph here?"

"Nope. He had to run to the hospital."

Shirley replaced the plate without asking why Ralph was working on a Saturday. All the girls were familiar with his off-hours responsibilities. "Evelyn said she might be running a little late. She had a hair appointment."

Anne smiled as Shirley moved to arrange the dishes and glasses around the kitchen table. It didn't matter if it was her house or one belonging to the others—a lot of problems had been solved around the kitchen table. Perhaps Shirley had sensed that this would be one of those times.

Anne dropped two large tea bags into the pitcher and covered them with boiling water. Immediately, the earthy scent of orange and black pekoe filled the kitchen. "Okay, I'm going to let those steep. Joy should be here any minute."

Several minutes later, the doorbell rang, followed by creaking as the door opened and a cheery "hello" floated down the hall.

"Come on in," Anne and Shirley called in unison.

Shirley swept out of the kitchen and returned with Joy in tow. "Look who I found."

Joy too had a platter in her hands. She pulled back the tinfoil on it to reveal mounds of golden cookies. "I couldn't sleep so I baked some white chocolate macadamia cookies. When you called this morning, I figured they would go great with our lunch."

"Right there," Anne said, pointing with the spoon she'd used to remove the teabags. "Next to Regina's brownies."

"Regina made brownies? Great." Joy groaned and rolled her eyes. "So much for Talia's classes helping me drop a few pounds. I'll probably gain them all back by the time lunch is over."

"Pooh. You always look fabulous." Stepping on the lever for the trash can, Anne disposed of the soggy teabags then added ice to the pitcher and set it alongside the chicken salad and bread already on the table. "Shall we start? Evelyn can join us when she gets here."

In fact, Evelyn was only a few minutes late joining them. She hurried in, her hair still damp on the tips. "Here I am. I came as soon as I could. You didn't talk about anything without me, did you?"

"Silly." Shirley pushed out Evelyn's chair with her foot and handed her the bread. "You know we would've filled you in."

"Yeah, but I thought of something while I was getting my hair cut." Evelyn plopped into the chair and took the bread from Shirley. "The video footage."

"What footage? I thought we didn't have any of the attacks," Anne said.

"Correct." Evelyn took a slice of bread and waved it at them. "Anybody stop to think why not?"

"Well…" Anne looked from Joy to Shirley. Both shrugged.

Evelyn set the bread plate down with a thump. "Either the attacker is extremely lucky and should plan a trip to Vegas or…"

Following her line of thought, Anne snapped her fingers. "Or they know where to look for the cameras!"

"Exactly." Evelyn gave a satisfied grunt, tore off a piece of the bread, and then leaned forward to rest her arms on the table while she ate it. "I'm thinking either they work there or someone has been scoping out the hospital while they plan these attacks."

Anne pushed her uneaten sandwich aside and started ticking off the suspects on one hand. "Okay, let's start with the hospital employees. There's Marilyn, for one. She has opportunity and motive."

"Right, but don't forget about Benny." Eyebrows raised, Evelyn looked at each of them in turn. "He was actually the person who came to mind first because of his temper."

"I'm not so sure about him," Joy said, twirling a lock of hair around her finger. "He has opportunity, yes, and as a janitor, he would know every inch of the hospital, including where all the cameras are, but what's his motive?"

She had a point. Anne frowned and Evelyn's shoulders sank a bit.

"There's also Preston." Much as she hated to include him, Anne couldn't quite rule him out. "He has more motive than either of the others, though I would say slightly less opportunity." She looked at Shirley. "What do you think?"

"Honestly?" Shirley shivered a bit and rubbed her hands over her arms. "I'd much rather think it was a random attack than a personal vendetta."

"Oh, Shirley." Joy leaned in close on one side, Evelyn on the other.

Anne could certainly understand how this could be upsetting for Shirley. What wasn't quite as clear was why she suddenly felt tears in her eyes.

She blinked and shoved up from the table. "This calls for chocolate. And sugar. Lots and lots of sugar."

She grabbed the brownies and cookies and carried them to the table. Fortunately, by the time she set them down, her eyes no longer burned. But deep down, the fear remained. And something else. Something she couldn't quite put her finger on. Something gnawing. Something...

Something she wasn't quite ready to face.

Chapter Eleven

Sunday was a day of rest, something Anne had realized she sorely needed as she'd sat in church, the words of the worship songs rolling over her in waves. More than once, she'd had to blink away tears, something she often saw in others but not so much in herself. She pondered this as she drove to work Monday, the song on the radio an echo of the one they'd closed the service with Sunday. She reached for the volume and turned up the music.

The song continued on, the words playing over and over in Anne's brain. Was it her longing for Ariane that made them so powerful?

She clicked off the radio and made the rest of the drive in silence. She couldn't think on that now. Today she needed to focus on the things happening at the hospital. Nothing else.

As she pulled into her parking spot, she thought about the attacks. After lunch the other day, the four of them had decided to check with security to see if they could have access to surveillance footage from the parking garage and the Grove. The possibility that they would find anything was slim, especially since Shirley had already looked at the Grove footage once and the police had been over it as well. Still, they were determined to pursue every avenue, and Shirley would be meeting Anne at the hospital before she began her volunteer duties.

The sky had just begun to tint orange above the palm trees as Anne walked along Mercy Street toward the hospital, and a gentle breeze stirred the edges of her collar. That was the thing about Charleston. It could be sharp and cold one day and border on balmy the next, especially in October. Today, it was the scent of adelia, canna lilies, and roses that mingled with the sea air blowing off the harbor that made Anne smile.

Inside, the hospital was already bustling. Anne had learned early on that Mercy never slept. Even in the wee hours of the morning, people scurried across the lobby or hopped on the elevators, and today was no exception. Shirley, however, was not among them.

Anne glanced at her watch. She still had fifteen minutes before the meeting time they had set. She could smell the bacon and sausage wafting from the kitchen, so she made a beeline in that direction in search of coffee.

She slowed as she entered the cafeteria. Dr. Seybold leaned against the coffee bar talking with a young intern. Except for the two of them and several nurses hunched around a table gobbling their breakfast, the rest of the place was empty.

Anne pulled a paper cup from the dispenser, but Dr. Seybold was completely engrossed in the woman he was talking to and didn't realize she couldn't reach the coffee.

"Excuse me." When they looked at her, Anne pointed to the carafes. "Would you mind if I just…?"

"Oh, sorry." The woman straightened with a jerk, grabbed her tray of eggs, toast, and juice, and moved out of the way. Dr. Seybold, however, grimaced and didn't say a word as he shifted to give her access.

"Thank you," Anne said, but he'd already returned his attention to the young woman.

"Anyway, as I was saying, Stephanie, if you haven't tried Bernie's, you really should. The food, the atmosphere—it's all amazing. They even have live music on the weekends if you like to dance."

"Oh, I do. Thanks, Dr. Seybold. I'll check it out."

"No problem. How 'bout Friday?"

"Um…" Stephanie blinked and dropped her gaze, her cheeks flushing pink. Her fingers looked red where she clutched the edges of her tray.

This was getting awkward. Anne filled her cup, anxious to leave the couple alone, but when Dr. Seybold had shifted away from the coffee, he'd blocked the condiments.

"I can pick you up if you want." He pulled his phone out of his lab coat pocket and held it out to Stephanie. "Give me your contact information, and I'll call you later this week so we can talk about it."

"Yeah, I suppose that would be all right." Her cheeks got redder as she set down the tray. She glanced at Anne as she took the phone and swiped, then pushed the phone back at him. "Uh, it's locked."

"Here, let me help you." He shoved away from the coffee bar and pressed close to Stephanie's side. Too close.

I'm out. Coffee creamer or no, Anne was uncomfortable with the entire situation. She snagged a lid, paid for the coffee, and then headed for the exit. One sip, and she regretted even stopping. It was old and bitter and had probably been sitting all night. She grimaced just as Shirley came in.

"Ah, I figured I'd find you here." Shirley pointed to her cup. "Think I'll get some of that too."

Anne grabbed her arm and swung her toward the door. "Trust me, you don't want it."

"Huh?" Shirley's brow wrinkled in confusion, but she followed Anne out. "What's going on?"

"Mercy's version of *The Dating Game*," Anne said. Tossing her coffee into a nearby trash can, she filled Shirley in on what she'd witnessed. "I mean, there's nothing wrong with the two of them flirting. He was obviously attracted to her, but with me standing right there? It was just weird."

"Hmm. That may be why Marilyn is trying so hard to find another job in a different department."

Anne raised her eyebrows, surprised the idea hadn't occurred to her before. "Do you think that's it?"

"Well, maybe. Marilyn has been Dr. Seybold's assistant for several years, but according to a couple of my friends, she's never really been happy there. She applied for two different positions last year but got passed over for one reason or another."

Shirley laid her hand on Anne's arm. "But that's not all. Early this morning, my friend called and told me the last position she applied for was in accounting."

Her tone and the intensity on her face said she was about to share something important.

Anne leaned closer. "Yeah?"

"The person who got it was Beatrice Whiting."

Anne's eyes widened as understanding dawned. "Your friend from church."

"Yep. The one I wrote a recommendation for and the one Marilyn said had a lot less experience."

"Good night, nurse!"

Suddenly, Marilyn's possible motive for targeting Shirley came into sharp focus. Anne covered Shirley's hand with her own.

"I just had an idea. Do you think you could talk to Seamus about reviewing the footage by yourself?"

"Of course, but what are you going to do?"

Anne checked the time on her watch. "I don't know when Dr. Seybold's office opens, but I think it'd be worthwhile to pay a visit to Marilyn, see if I can learn more about her—what she's like, how she feels about her job, stuff like that."

Shirley nodded. "That sounds good. Let me know what you find out."

Anne gave Shirley a hug and then hurried toward the elevators. Dr. Seybold's office was on the fourth floor, along with cardiac and cardiac ICU. She quickly found his name on the board directory and followed the signs until she stood outside his door. But what exactly would she ask once she was inside?

She took a moment to collect her thoughts before pushing open the door and stepping in. Marilyn sat behind a pale, ash-colored desk, the phone pressed to her ear and a frown on her face. Behind her on the wall was a large board bearing Dr. Seybold's name with the words CARDIAC SURGEON in flowing script underneath. Except for a spiky plant in a plain white vase, the rest of the space was bare. And the room was oddly devoid of smell. Not even a hint of perfume or air freshener. Plus there were no pictures or personal effects to be seen anywhere. Was this a sign of Marilyn's unhappiness, or did the doctor not allow such novelties?

Marilyn covered the receiver with her hand and whispered to Anne, "I'll be right with you. Go ahead and have a seat." She nodded to a sleek black leather sofa pushed against the wall then went back to her phone call.

"Listen, Estelle, I drop off the doctor's dry cleaning every Thursday. There are always four lab coats and three pairs of scrubs. This morning when I picked them up, there were only three lab coats. Everything else was there."

She listened a moment, the tapping of the letter opener in her other hand against the desk a clear sign of her irritation.

"I'm absolutely certain. I checked the bag myself."

More tapping, this time accompanied by a sigh.

"Okay. Please do what you can. I'll check back with you this afternoon. Thank you."

She hung up, scribbled something on a sticky note, and then rose and crossed to a narrow closet. Inside was a plastic dry cleaner's bag with ESTELLE'S FASHION CLEANERS stamped across the front.

Marilyn stuck the note to the bag then closed the door and turned to Anne. "Sorry about that."

"No problem." Anne smiled and motioned to the closet. "Dr. Seybold has you pick up his dry cleaning?"

Marilyn snorted as she went back to her desk. "Among other things. I do a lot of stuff for him that doesn't necessarily fall under my job description, but do you think he appreciates it?"

Anne guessed the answer was no, but thought it better not to say so. "Some people can be oblivious that way."

"I suppose." Marilyn plopped into her chair then grabbed the edge of the desk and rolled herself forward. "What can I do for you? Did you have an appointment today?"

She opened a desk drawer and slid out a pair of reading glasses then perched them on the tip of her nose and ran her finger across the dates on her desk calendar, several of which were highlighted. The calendar itself had seen better days, with pages that were frayed and torn.

"No, actually, I stopped by to chat with you," Anne said. "Do you have a minute?"

"Me?" Marilyn laid the glasses aside and tucked a lock of ruddy brown hair behind her ear. "Wait, is this about the other day?"

"Um…sorry?"

"Outside Julie's office." Marilyn leaned back in her chair, the leather creaking softly. "I suppose you heard what I said to her?"

"I heard some," Anne admitted. Though this wasn't what she'd planned to say, it did provide her the opening she needed to ask about Marilyn's current position with the hospital. "You sounded pretty unhappy."

"Wouldn't you be?" She snatched up the letter opener and resumed the agitated tapping against the desk. "I've worked at this hospital for almost eight years. I get to work on time and I hardly ever call in sick. Yet when it comes time for a promotion, I get passed over for girls half my age. My husband passed away four years ago. I live on one salary. I could really use the extra income."

Bombarded by the flood of information, Anne blinked and swallowed nervously. "I'm sorry to hear about your husband, Marilyn. I had no idea."

The tapping slowed, and the firm line of her lips softened a touch. "Thank you."

Anne pushed to the edge of the sofa. "Have you thought about asking HR why you keep getting passed over? Maybe taking a couple of classes would improve your résumé and—"

To Anne's shock, Marilyn flicked the sharp side of the letter opener down and jabbed it against the desk calendar. "I know why I keep getting passed over. I told you. It's because they want to hire people who are younger. Never mind if they have experience, or if they can do the job. At Mercy Hospital, it's all about looks."

Jabs punctuated each word, widening the tears on the page. At least now Anne knew what had caused them.

"I'm sure that's not true, Marilyn," she said, the scripture from Proverbs "*a gentle answer turns away wrath*" circling in her brain.

Marilyn sat back and crossed her arms, her fingers drumming on her crossed arms. "No? What about this last girl, Beatrice Whiting?"

"To be honest, I don't know Beatrice—" Anne began. She got no further. Marilyn launched into a tirade that bordered on belittling. Finally, Anne could listen no more. She held up her hand.

"I'm really sorry you're upset, Marilyn. You may very well have good cause to be so, but right now, I think the best thing would be for you to talk to Dr. Seybold and let him know why you're unhappy."

Anne was careful to keep her tone and volume soft and her words encouraging. As angry as Marilyn appeared, anything less would only make matters worse. Thankfully, she seemed to calm a bit. She uncrossed her arms and her chin didn't jut quite as far.

"You're right, I guess. I'm just mad and…"

"Hurt?" Anne suggested.

Marilyn yanked open the same desk drawer where she'd gotten the glasses and took out a pack of travel tissues. After pulling one loose, she pressed it to her nose and blew. "I know it sounds stupid, but I just want to feel appreciated for what I do," she said between sniffles.

"It's not stupid, Marilyn," Anne said, relieved to see her anger subsiding. "We all want to know we're valued by the people we work for. In fact, the way you're feeling is pretty common."

She met and held Anne's gaze over the tissue, as though unsure whether she could believe what Anne said and was therefore not quite ready to trust her. Finally, she balled up the tissue and tossed it into a shiny metal wastebasket.

"You're probably right. Anyway, thanks for stopping by. I appreciate you coming to talk to me."

"You're welcome. And, Marilyn, my husband Ralph is the chaplain here. I'm sure he would love to meet with you if you need someone else to talk to."

To Anne's dismay, the hardness brought on by anger returned to Marilyn's face as she shook her head.

"Thanks, but I'm okay. It may not look like it at the moment, but I have things under control."

That was hardly the picture Anne saw. In fact, Marilyn looked anything but under control. But did that mean she was capable of attacking her fellow coworkers?

The question formed an uneasy knot in the pit of Anne's stomach as she left Dr. Seybold's office, a knot she knew wouldn't go away until they'd found their culprit. And that was something they had to do soon.

Before anyone else got hurt.

Chapter Twelve

ANNE SLOWED HER STEPS OUTSIDE the volunteer office the next morning, surprised to hear Aurora's voice raised as though she were berating someone. That "someone" turned out to be Polly Periwinkle, a friend and longtime hospital volunteer.

"Polly?" Anne asked, as Polly swung out of Aurora's office, her face flushed and angry. "Is everything okay—?"

Polly raised her hand to cut Anne off and kept walking. A split second later, Aurora also stormed out but refused to look at her.

What was going on? Enough of this. Time to find out.

Anne hurried down the hall and spotted Aurora just as she was stepping onto the elevator.

"Hey, can you hold the door?"

Though she didn't look pleased, Aurora held her finger to the button until Anne joined her.

"What just happened back there?" Anne asked. "Is everything okay?"

Aurora took a deep breath and puffed it out. "It was nothing."

"It didn't look like nothing. Polly was so mad, I thought I saw steam coming out of her ears."

The elevator arrived on the first floor, and the doors opened with a soft hiss. For a moment, Anne thought Aurora might storm off without answering. Instead, she hesitated, then leaned against the back of the elevator and let the doors slide closed.

"Polly was upset because I had to change the schedule."

Schedule changes were commonplace. That alone wouldn't have been enough to inspire the kind of reaction Anne had witnessed. She shook her head. "I don't understand."

Aurora dropped her gaze, one foot shuffling over the other in a move that resembled nervousness.

Filled with sudden compassion, Anne touched Aurora's arm. "I don't know what's been going on, but I'm here if you'd like to talk about it."

Aurora looked up, her eyes filling with sudden tears. Sucking in a breath, Anne pushed the button to return the elevator to the volunteer office. Once there, she crossed to the supply closet and took out a box of tissues and set it on the desk. "Let's talk."

Ripping the top off the box seemed to calm Aurora's nerves. She threw the scrap of cardboard away and then slid the box to Anne. "Thanks, but I think I'm okay now."

"Good. I'm glad. But I still think talking about what's had you in such a tangle the last few days will help."

It took a minute, but Aurora finally agreed.

Anne sank into a chair opposite the desk and waited, a trick she'd learned from Ralph when he wanted a person to open up. After several long seconds, it worked.

"It's about David," Aurora said at last.

Anne blinked. "I'm sorry, who?"

"My boyfriend. I don't talk about him much because, well, let's just say we've had our ups and downs."

Anne didn't even realize Aurora had a boyfriend, but saying so might seem rude. She motioned for Aurora to continue.

Very slowly, Aurora reached for a tissue and pulled it out of the box. In the quiet office, even this gentle scrape seemed loud. She drew the tissue close and began tearing pieces off the edge. "One of the things that's been hard for us to overcome is our careers. David wants to move to Detroit. My job is here. But a couple of weeks ago, the job he wanted became official. Now I have to decide if I want to go with him."

Leave the hospital? Anne tried to hide her surprise but probably failed miserably. "That's a huge decision."

"I know." Aurora sighed then continued talking, sharing parts of her life and David's that Anne found unexpected. And a little convicting. How was it that she knew so little about Aurora's life outside the hospital? Granted, she wasn't one to share details. Still, caring about people meant taking the time to get to know them.

"I'm sorry that I didn't know any of this before now," Anne said when Aurora finished. "I'll certainly be praying for you while you make your decision."

"Thanks." She sniffled and swiped the tissue under her nose. "I would appreciate you praying for us later this week. David and I are going to Detroit to check out the area, meet with his prospective employer, stuff like that. We've already made a couple of quick trips, but now that they've extended an offer, we need to get serious about checking out the location, finding two apartments close together."

Which explained her sensitivity to schedule changes. When she couldn't find a sub, Aurora covered the shift herself. Obviously, that wouldn't be possible if she was in Detroit.

"Do you need someone to cover Polly's shift?" Anne asked, carefully. She didn't want Aurora to think she was meddling.

"That would be nice." Aurora's face fell guiltily. "I kinda blew up when Polly told me she had to be out this week. I didn't handle it very well."

"Why don't I cover for you while you give her a call?" Anne suggested. "I'm sure the two of you can work it out."

She rose and headed for the door. When she looked back, Aurora was already reaching for the phone. Well, that was one problem solved. Or at least part of it. Aurora still had a decision to make, one that would affect them all.

The thought weighed heavily as Anne went about her duties. But even more pressing was the desire to talk to Shirley—tell her about the conversation with Marilyn and find out if she'd learned anything from the surveillance video. Evelyn and Joy would need to be filled in too, only before she could do any of that, she needed to walk several patients down to discharge and then make the rounds to the departments. And let Ralph know she'd be working late a couple of nights to cover Polly's shifts.

She was so caught up in her thoughts that she didn't even hear Shirley calling her name until she was almost at her elbow.

"Anne, there you are. I've been looking all over the hospital for you." A thin sheen of sweat coated Shirley's face, even with the paper fan she waved under her chin.

Shirley was so excited that she looked like a bird, hopping from foot to foot and fanning so fast Anne thought she might lift off the floor.

"What's going on?" She looked past Shirley down the hall and back. "Did you find something? Was there something on the video? What?"

"It *was* the video. I didn't notice it before because there were a lot people coming and going from the Grove. But this time, instead of looking for something suspicious, I just watched the video, same as I would if were watching a movie."

"And?" Anne's heart had begun beating fast, and she matched Shirley's motion of hopping from foot to foot. "Shirley, what is it? What did you see?"

"Not what…who. I saw Preston, Anne. Preston was in the Grove. And it was just a few minutes before I was attacked."

Chapter Thirteen

Preston was in the Grove? But that didn't mesh with what Anne thought about Marilyn. Anne frowned. "Shirley, are you sure?"

"Positive." Shirley quit bouncing and looked Anne in the eyes. "What? I thought we wanted evidence. You sound like you're upset that it's about Preston."

"Well, not upset. Just confused. Him being in the area isn't exactly hard evidence." Anne told her about the conversation with Marilyn, and how angry she'd seemed at first, an emotion that had changed until it became calm and almost calculating. "At least, that's how it appeared," Anne said. "I was actually super excited to talk to you about it because I wanted your opinion on whether or not you thought she'd be capable of hurting one of her coworkers."

Shirley's chin jutted obstinately at first, but bit by bit the line of her jaw softened until she no longer looked so certain. "Well, I mean, I suppose anybody could be capable of anything, given the right motivation," she admitted when Anne finished.

And there it was. They'd circled all the way back to motivation. Anne sighed and shoved her hands into the pockets of her volunteer smock. "I guess there's nothing for it. We're going to have to figure out what Preston was doing at the hospital the night of the attack and if he has an alibi for when it happened. The question is how. I don't even know where he lives."

"We could search for him on the internet. If that comes up empty, we could check with Julie," Shirley said. "If he's been sending letters to the hospital, surely she's seen an address."

"Good point." Anne thought a moment, then nodded. "Yes, I like that idea. I just took my last patient down to discharge. Should we go now?"

Shirley grimaced. "I can't. I told Mama I would be home thirty minutes ago, but I wanted to find you first."

"Okay. You go on home. I'll talk to Julie."

"But call me when you're done?"

"Of course. In the meantime, would you mind letting Evelyn and Joy know what's going on?"

"Will do."

Anne wrapped Shirley in a quick hug and then the two of them parted, with Anne heading in one direction and Shirley going the opposite. Upstairs, Julie was saying goodbye to Talia.

"So, you'll be at class tonight?" Talia asked, running her finger along the length of her necklace.

"I will. See you later."

"Okay, bye." Talia spun, spotted Anne, and smiled at her as she passed. "Anne, right?"

"That's right. How are you, Talia?"

"Doing great." She smiled again, added a wave, and swung out the door.

Anne turned to Julie. It didn't take her long to tell her what she wanted, but Julie seemed hesitant to give her the information.

"It's not that I don't trust you, Anne. Of course, I do, but patient privacy…" She raised both hands and shrugged. "It's hospital policy. There's not a whole lot I can do."

"I completely understand, Julie. I wasn't even thinking about policy when I came up here." She laughed and tapped her temple. "One-track mind, and all that."

Julie nodded. "I get it. I'm like that too sometimes." She hesitated and rubbed one hand along her jaw. "So…do you mind if I ask why you want Preston's address?"

Anne sucked in her bottom lip. So far, she'd managed to avoid telling Julie about her suspicions, but she couldn't exactly ask her for a favor and then refuse to tell her why.

"It's sort of complicated," she began, but cut off when the door swung open behind her and a man charged into the office.

Julie's eyes widened, resembling two pale blue saucers in her small face. "Mr. Winder. What can I do for you?"

Preston Winder wore a dark jacket, unzipped, with a pair of wrinkled khakis that looked like they could use washing, and a plaid shirt partially untucked. Under his arm was a bundle of papers shoved helter-skelter into folders. "Is Mr. Baker in?"

"He is, but…" Julie flipped the pages on her desk calendar. "Were you, um, did you have an appointment, Mr. Winder?"

He widened his stance and thrust out his chin. "Do I need an appointment to see what is being done about my son's case?"

He grabbed one of the folders, leaned forward, and tossed it onto Julie's desk, scattering the papers inside.

"Oh." Julie fell silent and stared, as taken aback as Anne felt. "Let me just…I'll see if Mr. Baker is available."

She jerked her thumb over her shoulder, then whirled and walked in the direction she'd pointed. After knocking once, Julie entered without waiting for Garrison to answer and slipped through the door.

Anne kept her gaze on Garrison's door, though from her peripheral, it was easy to see that Preston had noticed her. She cleared her throat and turned to him.

"I'm Anne Mabry, one of the volunteers here at the hospital."

He studied her a second longer then turned his attention to the door. Anne's gaze fell to the papers strewn across Julie's desk. They were letters, or copies of them, all with Preston's address printed in the header.

1514 Lambright.

Anne swallowed and tore her gaze away. She wanted to speak to Preston, tell him how sorry she was about his son, but would that be wrong since she was affiliated with the hospital? And what if he was behind the attacks? No, that didn't matter. As one parent who'd lost a child to another, she could at least offer comfort.

"Mr. Winder—"

Garrison's door swung open and both he and Julie walked through. Anne took a step back. Garrison's eyes registered her presence for a split second before he focused on Preston.

"Mr. Winder, Julie tells me you've got some questions about your son's case."

"Not just questions. I want to know what *you're* doing about the mistakes your staff made regarding his care."

To his credit, Garrison remained calm in the face of Preston's raised voice and jabbing finger. He lifted both hands, palms out.

"Mr. Winder, you know hospital staff are not allowed to speak with you while the litigation is ongoing. I can tell you we've done a thorough investigation and—"

"Investigation. Bah!" He jerked the rest of the papers out from under his arm and shook them in Garrison's face, several newspaper clippings and other things fluttering to the floor. "You call what you've been doing an investigation? It's a travesty, is what it is. My son *died* while in your care!"

His voice rose with every syllable, and so did Preston. He stretched himself to his full height, which was considerable, until he towered over Garrison and poor Julie, who looked like she might faint at any moment.

"Mr. Winder, I'm afraid I'm going to have to ask you to leave." Garrison lowered his voice a notch. "This is still a workplace."

"That's another thing. Do your *patients* know they're risking their lives by coming here? Have you told them you won't do a thing to find out what happened if one of them dies?"

"I understand you're upset," Garrison began.

"Upset! Ha! That's a laugh." He threw the papers down, or maybe he threw them at Garrison. Either way, Garrison looked angrier than Anne had ever seen him.

He walked back around the desk, all semblance of patience gone. "I'm going to call security."

For several seconds, no one spoke, and then Preston scowled and raked his fingers through his hair. "That won't be necessary. I'm through here."

He whirled and stomped to the door, leaving it gaping as he stormed out. Anne sagged with relief once he was gone. It was as though Preston's presence had sucked all the air out of the room and it only just returned when he left.

"Wow." She looked at Julie and then at Garrison. "Have y'all had to deal with that before?"

"It's been getting worse the last few weeks." Garrison turned to Julie, who still looked pale. "Why don't you take the rest of the afternoon off?"

She didn't need to be told twice. She grabbed her keys and her purse and made a beeline for the exit.

Her sweater was still draped across the back of her chair. Anne circled around and grabbed it. "Julie, your sweater?"

She nodded but didn't bother returning for it. Gauging by the redness of Julie's eyes, Anne could see she was on the verge of tears and wouldn't be able to hold them back much longer.

"Sorry you had to see that," Garrison said after Julie had gone. He stepped to the reception desk and began scraping the papers and folders into a pile.

"It's a tough situation all around," Anne replied. "I'm sorry you and Julie have to deal with it."

She crouched to pick up the papers that had spilled onto the floor. Among them were several newspaper clippings about the muggings that had taken place at the hospital. Why would Preston have them, and what was he trying to say by bringing a copy of them to Garrison?

She rose to give the papers to Garrison, who took them with a frown and slid everything into a drawer then locked it.

"I'll deal with that stuff later. Right now, I need to call our legal team and let them know we've had another visit from Mr. Winder and talk about getting a restraining order."

It was a drastic step, but judging by the scene she'd just witnessed, Anne feared it was a necessary one.

"I'll let you get to it," Anne said. "And I'll be praying for you, Garrison."

Weariness fell over him like a shroud, bending his shoulders and adding lines to his face. "Thanks, Anne. I would appreciate that."

She turned for the door, already asking the Lord to give Garrison the wisdom he would need to see this situation through. Certainly it was a trying time for them all. The question was, how would they hold up under the pressure? How would Preston hold up? And how far would he go to get what he wanted?

No, that wasn't right. The real question was, how far had he already gone?

Chapter Fourteen

ANNE DROVE SLOWLY THROUGH THE streets of downtown Charleston, occasionally glancing at her phone as she followed the instructions from her navigation. Dusk came early this time of year, which made reading the street names harder, but eventually she found the one she wanted.

Streetlamps lit the length of Lambright from one to the other. Any other evening, Anne might have slowed to admire the charming homes with their colorful fall displays, but not tonight. As she'd promised, she'd called Shirley after she left Garrison's office but hadn't told her she'd decided to drive past Preston's house on her way home from work. In her own defense, it wasn't planned. The idea popped into her head when she got into the car. And what possible harm could come from looking to satisfy her curiosity?

Lambright was quite a long street, and Anne had to pass several one-story brick structures with carefully landscaped yards before she came to number 1514. Like the houses on either side, this one was traditional in style, but the trailing hibiscus around the door needed to be cut back, and one of the shutters had gone askew. The grass also looked like it hadn't been mowed in some time and had even gone to seed in spots. At least it appeared so with the setting sun casting long shadows across the lawn.

Anne took her foot off the gas and let the car slow to a crawl. No light shone through the mullioned windows or door. No porch light cast a welcoming glow. In fact, the house looked vacant, with its dark, staring eyes and dead or dying landscaping. Could it be she'd typed the address wrong into her phone?

She reached out to take it from the cup holder, but a glimpse of a figure through the windshield made her screech and slam on the brakes. The car rocked to a stop. A second later, the automatic headlights flickered on, shining brightly against the silver zipper of Preston's coat. Without a word, he circled around to the driver's side.

Breathing hard, Anne hit the button to roll down her window. "Mr. Winder, you startled me. I didn't see you standing there. Are you all right?"

But he wasn't there a moment ago. She was sure of it. And what was he even doing lurking in the middle of the street?

"Didn't I see you at the hospital?" he asked, ignoring her question.

"Um…"

He wagged his finger at her, the keys in his hand jingling. "Mr. Baker's office, this afternoon. I saw you."

"Yes, that was me."

"Did you follow me home?"

What kind of question was that? He'd left the hospital hours ago. "No, actually I just got off work."

"You followed me."

His habit of asking a question and then punctuating it with an accusing statement raised the hackles on Anne's neck.

"No, sir, I wasn't following you. I was curious about you, though," she admitted, careful not to say too much. "You were very upset when you came by the hospital earlier today."

He crossed his arms and glared at her. "So you came by to spy on me? What did you think you were going to see?"

That was a tough question to answer. "I'm not sure." Anne tried her best to appear bold and self-assured, even though she was quaking in her shoes. "I suppose I just wanted to know a little more about you."

Her honesty seemed to take him back. He clamped his mouth shut and narrowed his eyes as he stared at her.

"I should probably be going," Anne said. Now that he'd calmed down some, she didn't want to risk making him mad all over again. "It's getting late. I'm sorry I bothered you and…I'm very sorry about your son."

She reached for the button to raise the windows. Pushing his keys into his coat pocket, he stepped closer and laid both hands over the opening on her door.

"What do you know about my son?"

All color drained from his clamped lips. Unable to tear her gaze away, Anne stammered, "Well, nothing. I mean, I know he passed away last year."

His grip on the door tightened, turning his knuckles as white as his lips. Anne's heart hammered against her ribs. She should go. Now.

"Who are you?" he asked, voice low. "How did you get my address?"

"I have to go, Mr. Winder. Please let go of my car."

He slapped the door with one hand. "Who sent you?"

Worried for her own safety, Anne took her foot off the brake and let the car ease forward. "Mr. Winder, I'm leaving," she said, more forcefully when he refused to let go and walked alongside her, repeating the question, "Who are you?"

Finally, his hands fell away and Anne sped up, her heart pounding now and her breath coming in shallow gasps. In the rearview mirror, Preston stood pointing at her wildly, his mouth a jagged line across his reddened face, and his voice echoing in the shadowy gloom of her taillights.

"I know you! Mabry! I know who you are. You're Anne Mabry!"

# Chapter Fifteen

ANNE'S NERVES WERE STILL SHOT as she rattled the key in the lock to her house. She jumped back as the door swung open, almost gasping in relief when she saw Ralph.

After seeing her face, he stepped onto the porch to grip her arms. "Honey, are you okay?"

"I'm fine now." She sank against his chest and let him hold her for a quiet moment before adding, "Let's go inside, and I'll tell you all about it."

Ralph's face remained stoic as they sat in the living room, where she told him about the visit with Preston.

"And how did he know your name?" he asked when she finished.

"That was earlier, at the hospital. I gave him my name and told him I was a volunteer."

Here, in the safety of her home, with the lights keeping the shadows at bay and her husband present, the last vestiges of nerves and outright fear melted away.

When she realized she was still clutching her purse, Anne leaned forward and set it on the floor. "I don't know, Ralph. The way he acted, I could easily see Preston being the person behind the attacks."

"If that's true, then we should call the police." He reached into his pocket and pulled out his cell phone, hesitating before he actually placed a call. "Except…"

"We don't have any proof," Anne finished for him. By now, he'd been around while she and her friends solved enough crimes to know the burden of evidence lay with them.

Ralph frowned and laid the phone on the coffee table. "Anne, I do not want you at the hospital late at night. It's not safe, especially if this guy is guilty, as you suspect."

Anne grimaced, and warmth flooded her face. "Well, now, that could be a problem. See, I already told Aurora I would pick up a few extra shifts later this week."

Ralph stared at her, mouth open and cheeks red. "You did what?"

"She told me about her boyfriend's job offer in Detroit. I'm guessing that's what she came to talk to you about?" she asked, talking quickly, before he could object. "I offered to help out before all of this happened with Preston."

A sigh puffed from Ralph's lips, but he didn't argue. "Fine. But we'll ride together so you aren't walking out to your car alone."

"I'll be working late, Ralph."

"I don't care. I don't want anything happening to you."

Affection for her husband rushed over her. She loved seeing this protective side of him, even if it wasn't practical. "You already work so hard and put in such long hours," she said softly. "Besides, I don't leave alone. The girls are with me. Plus we're working on getting all the proof we need to put an end to this for good. And speaking of the girls…"

She took out her phone and sent them a brief text. NEED TO MEET. CAN Y'ALL COME OVER?

Three pings from answering messages followed in short order. Anne smiled and showed her phone to Ralph.

"See? All under control."

"Huh." He grimaced and pushed up off the couch.

Still smiling, Anne went into the kitchen to make herself and Ralph sandwiches and put on a pot of coffee. By the time her friends arrived, it had finished brewing.

"What's all this about?" Evelyn took off her coat and hung it on a hook next to Joy's.

"Is this about Preston?" Shirley asked.

Anne looked at Shirley but pointed to Evelyn and Joy. "Did you tell them?"

"She called," Joy said. "She said he was in the footage from the Grove the night she was attacked."

"That's enough to make me suspicious," Evelyn said, a scowl forming on her face.

"You may be more than just suspicious when I tell you what happened today." Anne motioned them into the kitchen, where each of them claimed a chair around the table. After hearing about the confrontation with Preston in Garrison's office, and then again later outside his house, Evelyn blew out a deep breath.

"Whew. Sounds to me like we know the name of our culprit."

"Do we though? Without any proof..." Anne lifted her hands and shrugged.

"Well, the attacks all took place around the same time. We could talk to a neighbor, see if he was home on the nights they happened," Evelyn suggested.

"Or if he was seen coming and going around that time," Joy added.

Anne sat up straight as another detail of her conversation with Preston struck.

Shirley leaned forward. "What is it, Anne? What are you thinking about?"

"His keys. Preston had his keys in his hand," Anne said. "I assumed he was just getting home because all of the lights were off, but what if he was leaving?" She glanced at the clock on the microwave then turned wide eyes to her friends. "It's just after eight. That means it was a little before seven when I went by his house."

"Do you think maybe he was going to the hospital?" Joy's eyes widened to match Anne's. "Should we call security and let them know?"

Torn with indecision, Anne frowned. "I don't know. We just said we didn't have any proof that Preston is guilty."

"Seamus is working tonight," Shirley said. "We could always warn him to keep an eye out in case Preston comes by."

"Yes." Anne wagged her finger at Shirley. "I like that idea. Will you call him?"

"I'll do it right now." Shirley left the table, her cell phone in her hand, and eased into the hall.

"Now, about those neighbors." Evelyn drummed her fingers on the tabletop. "What street did you say Preston lives on?"

"Lambright. 1514 Lambright," Anne repeated. "I read it on the letterhead he gave to Julie."

Evelyn's face puckered into a scowl. "Why is that name so familiar?" She looked at Joy. "Does it sound familiar to you?"

Joy thought a moment and then shook her head. "I don't think so."

Evelyn sighed and scratched her head. "I just know I've heard it—I've got it!" She snapped her fingers then pointed at Anne. "Lambright is where Dorothy Baxter lives."

Shirley walked back into the kitchen. "What are we talking about? Who's Dorothy Baxter?"

"She's an older woman from church. She doesn't like to drive in bad weather, so every now and then she'll call and ask me for a ride. And she lives on Preston's street." Evelyn arched a brow. "Did you get ahold of Seamus?"

Shirley held up her phone. "Yep. Everything's good there."

"All right, then I'll call Dorothy, see what I can find out." Evelyn took her cell out of her purse, but instead of stepping into the hall as Shirley had done, she dialed, laid the phone on the table, and turned on the speaker. After a couple of rings, Dorothy answered.

Evelyn leaned closer. "Hey, Miss Dorothy, it's Evelyn."

"Yes, dear, how are you?"

"I'm doing fine. Do you have a minute to talk? My friends and I would like to ask you a few questions."

"Oh? Hold on a second. Let me turn down the TV."

"Of course, go ahead."

They heard Dorothy muttering as she looked for the remote and then she returned a moment later. "Evelyn, are you there?"

"Yes, ma'am. We have a couple of questions about Preston Winder. He lives down the road from you?"

"Winder? Yes, I know the Winders. They live in the brick house with the beautiful hibiscus vines around the front door."

Evelyn looked questioningly at Anne. She nodded.

"Yes, that's the place," Evelyn said. "Miss Dorothy, how well do you know Mr. Winder?"

"Goodness, not well. He doesn't get out much. He and his wife lost their son last year, you know."

"Yes, we'd heard about that."

"Just tragic what that poor family has gone through," Dorothy continued. In the background, a dog barked. "Pardon me, dear," she said. "I need to go and see what has Buster so riled up."

"Yes, ma'am. We'll wait," Evelyn said.

They heard Dorothy's phone rattle as she set it down. Finally, the dog stopped barking and Dorothy came back on the line.

"Silly dog. Always barking at squirrels. Anyway, what did you want to know about Preston?"

"Well, you may have already answered our question," Evelyn replied. "You said he doesn't go out much?"

"Oh no. Hardly ever. His car just sits there in the driveway, day after day. I see it on my way to my knitting circle."

"Uh-huh. What about in the evenings? Do you ever see his car then?"

"Funny you should mention it," Dorothy said.

Anne sucked in a breath. Next to her, Joy and Shirley did the same.

"For the last couple of weeks or so, I haven't seen his car in the evenings. But in the morning, it's always there. I can't imagine he got a job working nights. Not much call for accountants at that time of day, I suppose."

Anne angled her head at Evelyn. "*Job?*" she mouthed.

"So, Miss Dorothy, do you mean to say Preston isn't working?"

"Oh no, dear. He either quit his job after his son passed away, or he lost it."

"You mean he was fired?"

"I couldn't say for certain. I just know that people say that's one of the reasons his wife left him. He just sat around the house, day after day. I heard she finally had enough and filed for a divorce."

Preston's story just kept getting worse. He already blamed the hospital for the loss of his son. Did he blame them for the loss of his job and wife too?

"Um..." Evelyn looked around at each of them and lifted her hand questioningly. Shirley shook her head. Joy did too. Anne hesitated. While she wanted to know more about his wife, something held her back. Finally, she shook her head.

"Okay, Miss Dorothy, I think that's all we wanted to know," Evelyn said. "Thanks so much for talking with us."

"It was my pleasure, dear. Oh, and if you wouldn't mind swinging by here on Sunday, I sure could use a ride. I hear it's supposed to rain all weekend."

"Yes, ma'am, I'll be glad to. Pick you up around nine?"

"That'll be fine. Bye now."

"Bye, Miss Dorothy." Evelyn hung up and then looked at Anne. "Well, I guess that answers our question about whether Preston was coming or going."

"But it doesn't tell us *where* he was going." Anne blew out a breath and shook her head. "Man, I can't help but feel sorry for the guy, you know?"

Joy agreed. "He's certainly had a rough go of it the last few months." She rubbed her hands over her arms. "Unfortunately, he appears to have more motive than anybody else we've talked about."

Anne thought the same thing. "All right then, if we all agree Preston at least appears to be our culprit, what's our next step? Do you suppose maybe we could track down his wife?"

"I don't know how we'd do that," Evelyn said. "Besides, what would we say? 'Do you think your estranged husband might be capable of attacking helpless hospital employees'?"

"Good point." Anne pinched her bottom lip, thinking. "I guess the only thing would be to try to discover where he's going every night."

"Assuming Seamus doesn't figure that out for us," Shirley said, tapping her phone. "He told me he'll call if Preston shows up."

"Okay, well, keep us posted."

"Will do." Shirley rose from the table, and Evelyn and Joy stood with her.

"It's getting late. We should probably be going," Evelyn said.

"Oh, but how is Addie doing?" Joy asked. "Is she feeling better?"

A flush crept over Evelyn's face. "Yeah, I meant to ask too. Have you heard from Lili?"

"Not since last night," Anne admitted. "I called to check on her, but Lili said she'd already gone to bed and didn't want to wake her. I'll try again in the morning."

"Let us know," Shirley said. "We're praying for her."

"Thanks, girls."

All three ladies filed down the hall, with Anne bringing up the rear. They each gave her a hug before slipping outside. With the deadbolt in place, Anne turned and leaned against the door.

What a day it had been. At this point, all she wanted was to take a hot shower and climb into her PJs. Maybe read a little before going to sleep. Yeah. A book would take her mind off things, help clear her head.

She pushed away from the door and trudged toward the bedroom. Interrupted by the buzzing of her phone in her pocket, she stopped and took it out to see who had texted her. It was Lili. The text was brief and to the point.

ADDIE IS REALLY SICK. WE'RE HEADING TO THE ER. CAN YOU MEET US?

All traces of weariness fled as Anne's pulse slammed into overdrive. "Ralph, come quick!" she called, scrambling to find her purse and jacket. When he appeared, she waved her phone at him. "It's Addie. Lili's taking her to the hospital. We have to go."

It had been a long day...and it wasn't over yet.

Chapter Sixteen

ANNE WOKE TIRED AND IRRITABLE Wednesday morning, likely due to lack of sleep the night before. She'd lain awake for hours after coming home from the hospital, visions of emergency room visits with Ariane and panicked calls to the doctor keeping sleep at bay.

"Why now, Lord? Why is this bothering me again after all this time?"

Next to her, Ralph rolled onto his side and mumbled, "Did you say something, hon?"

"It's nothing. Go back to sleep." Easing out from under the covers, Anne checked the clock on the nightstand. Four thirty. It wouldn't be daylight for a couple of hours yet.

She padded out of the bedroom and down the hall without flicking on the lights. When she got to the living room, the glow from the satellite receiver cast just enough of a glimmer to save her shins as she wound around the couch and coffee table and turned on a lamp.

This time of day, even the ticking of the mantel clock sounded loud. Every creak and howl from the wind outside echoed in the rafters. But today, Anne didn't mind. She wanted the quiet to think. And pray. She grabbed a blanket from the arm of the couch and wrapped it around herself as she sat down.

I don't know what I'm feeling, Lord.

She closed her eyes. *I'm having a hard time understanding what's happening to me. Will You show me?*

No answer came. Anne opened her eyes and watched the gray shadows caused by the swaying of the tree limbs outside the window creeping across the floor.

Hot tears burned the insides of her eyelids. She blinked them back. "Every day I ask You to take care of my family and friends. But I—"

She broke off, afraid to voice what was in her heart.

Addie was still in the hospital, recovering from an emergency appendectomy. What if it had been something worse? What would have happened if they had waited any longer to take Addie to the ER?

"I'm so thankful Lili took her to the hospital."

It was a beginning. Anne had learned long ago the best way to feel better was to pray about the things she was grateful for. While the words were slow in coming, eventually she found them. And they spilled faster and faster from her lips.

"I'm thankful there was a doctor on call who could do the surgery. I'm thankful that there was no infection. And I'm *so* thankful that Ralph was there to keep me calm. Lord, I'm so glad this happened now, and not when Lili was deployed. There were days we couldn't reach her. Thank You that she was here, with Addie. And for Shirley…"

She stopped to wipe away the tears rolling down her face. The house was still silent, but it no longer felt empty. God was here, offering strength and comfort. In the drawer of the end table was a small Bible. Anne took it out and opened to one of her favorite passages of scripture.

I will lift up mine eyes unto the hills, from whence cometh my help. My help cometh from the LORD, which made heaven and earth. He will not suffer thy foot to be moved: he that keepeth thee will not slumber. Behold, he that keepeth Israel shall neither slumber nor sleep. The LORD is thy keeper: the LORD is thy shade upon thy right hand. The sun shall not smite thee by day, nor the moon by night. The LORD shall preserve thee from all evil: he shall preserve thy soul. The LORD shall preserve thy going out and thy coming in from this time forth, and even for evermore.

Comforted by the words, Anne stood and turned for the kitchen. She felt better having spent time with the Lord, and yet... was there something else? She paused in the doorway, one hand on the jamb. What else could there be? She'd told the Lord everything she'd been hiding.

Clearing her thoughts with a shake of her head, Anne moved on to the kitchen. One cup of coffee later, Ralph joined her, still rubbing the sleep from his eyes as he padded to the cupboard for a cup.

"How long have you been up?"

"A while." Anne smiled and joined him at the coffeepot for a refill.

"Have you heard from Lili?"

Sleep still roughened his voice. Anne smiled and rubbed his back and shoulder. "Not yet. I'm going to wait another thirty minutes and then give her a call."

"Okay." Ralph's mouth stretched in a yawn. "Let me know when you've heard how Addie is doing, will you?" He set down the mug and headed toward the door.

Anne lifted the pot. "You don't want any?"

"Nope. I'm going back to bed," he said, scrubbing his knuckles through his tousled hair.

Anne replaced the pot with a grunt. "Lucky. I wish I could go back to bed."

"I heard you," he called over his shoulder.

"I hope so," she teased, and then sighed. Enough dawdling. She needed to shower and dress and then get over to the hospital if she wanted to visit with Addie before her shift started.

An hour later, she walked down the hall of the pediatric floor, a mylar balloon attached to a bouquet of flowers bobbing above her head. Outside Addie's door, someone had placed a fluffy brown teddy bear on a chair. Tucked under one arm was a card. It read simply, *Get well soon, from your friends at Mercy.*

Anne smiled and picked up the bear, then poked her head into Addie's room. Lili was curled up in a chair, sound asleep, but Addie's eyes lit when she spied Anne.

"Nana!"

Anne put her finger to her lips and tiptoed into the room. "Morning, sweetheart. How are you feeling?"

"Better." When she spotted the bear, Addie struggled to push up from her pillows. "Is that for me?"

"It is, but only if you lie still and get some rest," Anne said.

Addie immediately lay down and held out her arms. Smiling, Anne put the teddy bear into them then set the flowers on the table next to the bed and pulled up a chair.

"So your mom's pretty tired, huh?"

"Yeah." Addie rolled her head to the other side to glance at her mother. "She kept waking up to check on me."

"Well, I can certainly understand why." Anne stroked Addie's hair. "We were pretty worried about you."

"Did you pray for me?"

Anne smiled and pressed a kiss to her forehead. "Of course, sweetheart. I always pray for you, even when you're not sick."

Addie giggled and squished the bear to her chin. "I'm glad you came to see me."

Warmth flooded Anne's heart. "I am too. Your grandpa will be stopping by later. Is there anything you want him to bring you?"

Addie smiled hopefully. "Ice cream?"

Anne laid her finger against her lips as though thinking it over. "Hmm. Not sure about that. We'll have to ask your doctor."

Addie frowned and turned her nose to sniff the bear. "I think I'm going to name him Gus."

Anne leaned forward to rub Addie's arm. "That's a funny name. What made you choose it?"

"I dunno. He looks like a Gus." She turned the bear's face to Anne. "Don't you think so?"

Anne pretended to study him. "You know, I think you're right. He does look like a Gus, especially around the eyes."

Lili stirred in the chair and then, as though remembering where she was, bolted upright and her gaze flew to Addie. "How do you feel, baby?"

"I'm okay. Nana's here."

"I see that." Gratitude softened the worried lines on Lili's forehead. "Hi, Mom. Thanks for coming."

"Of course." Anne rose and circled around the bed to give Lili a hug. "I tried calling earlier but it went straight to voice mail."

"Did you?" She rubbed her hand over her face. "My battery must be dead. I didn't grab my charger when we left the house."

"I can bring one by later. And what about clothes? Do you want me to run by the house and pick something up? Or if you want, I can sit with Addie so you can go home and shower."

Lili shook her head before Anne could finish. "I don't want to leave Addie. But if you could run by the house and grab a few things, that would be great."

"Sure, honey. Just make me a list. I'll do it as soon as I get off work."

"Thanks, Mom." Lili's eyes misted, but she turned her face away to compose herself, and when she looked back, there was no trace of tears. "And thanks for coming so fast last night. I was pretty scared when I couldn't figure out what was wrong with Addie."

"We all were. I'm just grateful that you brought her to the ER when you did. The surgeon said if you'd waited any longer, her appendix could have ruptured."

"What does ruptured mean?" Addie asked.

"It means it could have burst," Lili said, swiping her thumb down her daughter's cheek. "And then we would have been in a whole mess of trouble."

Addie seemed to think on this, but only for a moment. She pushed the bear toward Lili. "Did you see my bear?"

"Yes. Did Nana bring that for you?"

"Not me. It was outside the door when I got here," Anne said. "Nana brought the flowers and balloon."

"Those are nice too," Addie said, her thoughtfulness making Anne smile.

She rounded the bed one more time and pressed another kiss to her granddaughter's forehead. "I should get to work, but I'll come by on my lunch break. Will that be okay?"

Addie nodded.

"Yes?"

"Yes."

"Okay then." Anne tucked the blankets around Addie, leaving room for the bear, and ran her fingers over her cheek. "I love you, sweetheart. I'm very glad you're okay."

"Love you too, Nana. Thank you for my balloon."

"You're welcome. Bye, Lili."

"Bye, Mom."

Anne walked to the door, sneaking one last peek at her girls before she closed it behind her. It was hard to leave. In her heart, she wanted to stay and listen to Addie giggle while she talked to her mom. She wanted to shower her with ice cream, teddy bears, and sweet kisses. But downstairs another patient waited to go home and as much as she wanted to stay, she was needed elsewhere.

Several people crowded the elevator when Anne got on. That wasn't unusual for this time of day. Between doctors making their rounds and visitors to the hospital, people often filled the cars. Anne watched a young pregnant woman juggle her purse and a tote bag and thought about what it must have been like for Lili going through her pregnancy without a husband. When the doors swished open, Anne got off and took several steps before realizing she was on the wrong floor. She spun around, but she was too late. The elevator doors had already closed.

"That's what I get for being distracted," she mumbled then walked to the door, pushed the down button, and stepped back to wait. And wait. And wait. She sighed and hit the button again, though little good it would do if it had to stop on every floor.

"What do you think you're doing? This is my floor."

"Not anymore it isn't. You've been reassigned."

Anne swung around to search for the source of the voices, but saw no one.

"What are you talking about? I handle this part of three and all of four."

She knew that voice. It was coming from one of the patient rooms. Benny Pierce? He sound irritated.

"Like I said, you've been reassigned."

"Why, you—" Words followed. Angry words.

"Listen, man, don't get mad at me. You got a problem with this, you take it up with the boss. I'm just doing what I'm told."

By now, Anne wasn't the only one curious about the conversation. A couple of nurses had overheard as well, and they had rounded the corner and stood peering at the room farthest down the hall.

"You better believe I'm going to talk to the boss," Benny said.

There was a loud clatter, as though he'd dropped something, and then Benny stormed into the hall, past the nurses, and straight at Anne.

Not her, she realized—the elevator. The doors opened and Benny stalked on, jabbed a button, and then stood looking at her, his face so red it made his blond hair look almost white. "Are you getting in?"

She shook her head. "No, thanks."

He let go of the button, and the doors slid closed a second time. Though it would make her late, Anne hurried down the hall to the room Benny had exited. Another janitor stood near the bathroom, scowling at a mop bucket that had been turned onto its side, spilling the contents and the scent of lemon into the hall.

The clatter she'd heard? Anne thought so, judging by the disgusted look on the janitor's face.

She moved into the room and reached for the handle on the bucket. "Here, let me help you."

"Oh no, ma'am. I can get it." The janitor rushed forward and took the bucket from her. "Watch your step now." He pointed to a puddle of dirty water. "Wouldn't want you to slip."

"Thank you, um…" Anne looked at the name patch sewn onto his uniform. "Rob."

The mop still lay on the floor. She picked it up and handed it to him. "I couldn't help but overhear what happened."

Rob grunted. "Yeah, that Benny. He's got quite the temper."

"And you said he was reassigned. Was that to another floor?"

Rob nodded and swished the mop through the puddle, then stuck it into the wringer and pushed down the handle. "That's right. His work is sloppy, and the nurses on this floor got tired of talking to him about it."

"What do you mean 'sloppy'?"

He pointed to the dirty water. "Case in point. We're supposed to change the water in the mop buckets regularly and sanitize after every wipe down. Or the trash cans." He motioned with the mop handle. "Sometimes, he'd forget to change the bags and then the nurses had to do it. Stuff like that. But every time they said something to him, he'd either get mad or storm off. Finally, they had enough and went to the boss."

"So they reassigned him to another floor? That hardly seems like a solution." The words were out before Anne could think better of them.

Rob shrugged and looked past her toward the hall, then back at Anne. "You didn't hear it from me, but the boss and Benny are old friends. I think maybe he owes the guy a favor and is just trying to help him out, you know? Especially now that the nurse who reported him is gone."

"You know who reported him?" Anne asked.

"Sure do. The same one who got attacked last week. Merchant, I think her name is."

Shock rippled through Anne at the name. "*Susan* Merchant?"

"That's her." Rob lifted the mop and let it splat onto the floor. "Funny stuff, eh? All that business? Someone could almost think it wasn't a coincidence."

That was exactly what Anne was thinking, and it was likely what the girls would think once she told them. Which would be soon. Because suddenly, Benny was right back on top of her suspect list.

Chapter Seventeen

"I AGREE, IT'S JUST TOO much of a coincidence." Joy pushed the salt-shaker across the cafeteria table to Evelyn, then turned back to Anne. The cafeteria was busy for a Wednesday, but they had managed to find a quiet corner away from everyone where they could talk. "Unless…" She frowned and bit her lip. "Did Rob tell you *when* Benny spoke to Susan?"

"He didn't know." Anne shoved her half-eaten salad out of the way and rested both elbows on the table. "But it would have to have been before she was attacked since she hasn't been to work since, right? Anyway, it shouldn't be too hard to find out for sure." She leaned forward until her face appeared on the cell phone screen propped at the center of the table. "What do you think, Shirley?"

Shirley's mom, Regina, had been a nervous wreck since the attack. Not wanting to upset her further, Shirley had decided to call in from home rather than leave her alone. "I think…"

Shirley checked over her shoulder then leaned in closer to the screen. "I mentioned something to the maintenance director about trash cans not being emptied a few days before I was attacked. What if he told Benny?"

Anne's breath caught. "That would make two of you."

"And if Crystal or one of the other victims made three…" Joy's eyes widened. "Shirley, do you think you could find out?"

"I could ask them. I'm sure I could get their numbers."

Evelyn held up her hand. "Hold on now, before we get too excited, what about Preston?"

"Well, Seamus said he never showed up at the hospital last night," Shirley said.

Evelyn frowned and picked at the plastic lid on her coffee cup. "Could we at least see if Dorothy was right about his wife filing for a divorce? I would look, but my computer is still on the fritz."

"I can do it." Anne frowned. "I think. Where do I start?"

"Court filings. I can walk you through it," Evelyn said.

"Okay, good." At least they had a plan, if not answers. Anne rubbed her hands together. "I've only got two more patients this afternoon, and then I'm free for the day. Will that work for you, Evelyn?"

"It should. I'll be finished with my filing by then. We could head to the library around five when I get off."

Anne nodded. "I think that's a good idea. Working on it here at the hospital might draw too much attention. Shirley and Joy, we'll let you know what we find."

"And I'll let you know when I've heard from the other victims," Shirley said.

Behind her, Regina shuffled into the picture. "Shirley, baby, I can't find my glasses."

The image wobbled as Shirley stood. "I'll help you, Mama. Gotta go, girls," she whispered a second before the screen went black.

"Okay, that's it for now, I guess." Anne grabbed her phone and slid it into her smock pocket. "Lord, please let us or the police find some answers soon."

"Amen to that." Joy stood and pressed her hand to her chest. "Something about this case has me losing sleep."

"Me too," Anne admitted, though as she walked away, she couldn't help but wonder, was it the case or something else that kept her up?

The question prickled as she went about her business for the day. Hard as she prayed about it, focus on the job eluded her, and she wound up having to apologize when she was late picking up the second patient for discharge. Aurora certainly wouldn't be pleased—

She froze in her tracks and glanced at her watch. It was Wednesday. She'd told Aurora she would cover for Polly today.

A groan rose in her throat as she changed directions and moved toward the volunteer office. She couldn't go back on her word. She and Evelyn would just have to go to the library when she finished here. But first, she needed to get Polly's assignments.

"I'm very sorry," Aurora was saying into her phone as Anne neared the office. "Yes, I understand, and I assure you, it won't happen again. Yes. All right. Thank you." She sighed and hung up.

Had someone already called to complain about her? Anne's chest tightened as she knocked lightly on the door.

"Come in."

Anne poked her head into the room. "Have you got a minute?"

"Of course."

Anne was surprised when Aurora jumped to her feet and rounded the desk to wrap her in a hug. "How is Addie?"

"Oh, uh, she's doing fine. Recovering, thank goodness." She returned Aurora's hug and added a pat.

"That's wonderful." She pulled back, her face twisting with concern. "Did she like the bear?"

That was from Aurora? The idea hadn't even occurred to her. Anne blinked and nodded. "She loved it. Thank you so much, Aurora."

"No problem." She waved dismissively and went back to her chair. "If there's anything else I can do, just let me know."

"I will. Thanks again." Anne hesitated and moved closer to the desk. "Listen, about this afternoon." She motioned to the phone. "I'm really sorry if I caused you any trouble. I admit, I've been a little distracted today."

"What?" Aurora glanced at the phone and back, then laid her hand over the receiver. "Oh, this? No, that wasn't about you."

"Oh." Anne let out a relieved breath.

Aurora sat forward. "And even if it was, I wouldn't expect you to apologize. You've got your hands full."

Anne smiled. "Okay. Thank you."

"No problem." She waited, her head angled curiously.

"I'm supposed to take Polly's shift today," Anne said.

Aurora sat up straight. "Are you sure you still want to do that? I can try to find someone else." The desk drawer rasped as she slid it open and took out a file.

"That's okay," Anne insisted. "I planned on staying late. And I can always run up and check on Addie between patients."

Aurora started to put the file back, hesitated, then started again. "Are you sure? I mean I could—"

"I'm sure," Anne said, holding up her hand. "And anyway, aren't you supposed to be heading to the airport?"

Aurora took her time closing the desk drawer. "Actually, David is going by himself this trip. We...uh...we decided it would be best to spend some time apart to consider our options." She ended on a hoarse note and her nose and eyes turned pink, like she was fighting not to cry.

What could Anne say that wouldn't sound like a platitude? Not, *it'll all work out.* She didn't know if it would. And not, *there are plenty of fish in the sea.* Even worse, *I'm sure it's for the best.* That one had made her want to punch something a time or two.

She raised her chin, met Aurora's gaze, and said simply, "I'm sorry."

Aurora went still and said nothing for a long moment. "Thank you for that."

Meaning, thanks for not trying to fix it. Anne offered a smile of commiseration, then jerked her thumb over her shoulder. "I'm gonna go. Is Polly's schedule on the board?"

She nodded.

"Okay. I'll take care of it. And Aurora? I'm praying for you."

This time, she didn't try to hide the tears that filled her eyes. "Thanks." She swiped her fingers across her lashes. "I'll take all the prayers I can get."

"You got it."

Anne smiled then let herself out of the office. She took a picture of Polly's schedule, texted Evelyn about the change in plans, and then went to meet Polly's first patient. Talia was in the elevator when Anne got on. She smiled and moved over to make room for Anne.

"What floor?" Talia asked, hovering her finger over the buttons.

"Five, please."

"Sure." The doors slid closed, and Talia glanced over at Anne. "How's it going? We missed you at class last night."

Anne had been so preoccupied with Addie and the case, she hadn't given the fitness classes a thought. "Oh, right. I've just been busy. I'm hoping to be there tomorrow night though."

"Awesome. We'll see you then."

Talia smiled and dropped her gaze. Anne did the same, first studying her shoes and then Talia's white sneakers. At last, the elevator stopped, the bell chimed, and she got off.

"See you, Anne. Have a good day."

"You too," she said, glancing up at the lighted numbers above the door. Fourth floor? That was cardiac and ICU. Was she visiting a patient? Anne would have to remember to ask when she saw her next. Talia was still new to the hospital and wouldn't have had a lot of opportunity to make friends. Maybe taking the time to express concern would help her feel welcome.

Her phone pinged inside her pocket. Anne took it out and read the message from Evelyn.

DO YOU WANT ME TO HEAD TO THE LIBRARY BY MYSELF?

PROBABLY BETTER, Anne typed back. IT'LL BE AFTER FIVE BEFORE I'M DONE.

OKAY. I'LL LET YOU KNOW WHAT I FIND.

Frowning, Anne replaced the phone in her pocket. Much as she'd wanted to look for the information herself, it was more important that they get it, even if she couldn't go.

The afternoon flew by quickly after that. Between patient responsibilities, Anne made time to check on Addie and pick up the list from Lili of the things she needed from the house. By five thirty, when her phone rang, she was more than ready for a break. Anne sank into a booth in the coffee shop and answered it.

"Hello?"

"Anne, it's Evelyn. Are you still at the hospital?"

"Uh-huh. I've got another thirty minutes left. What did you find? Anything on Preston's wife?"

"Sure did. It's official. She filed for a divorce three weeks ago. It took me a while to find out because I didn't know the time frame at first."

"So Dorothy was right."

"Yep."

The news didn't make her happy.

"Have you heard from Shirley?" Evelyn asked.

"Not yet. If we still haven't by the time I get home, I'll call her."

"Okay. Anything you want me to do in the meantime?"

"I don't think so." Anne thought a second, then shook her head. "No, other than try to figure out what our next step with Preston will be. I suppose I could always talk to Julie in the morning and see if he's made any more trips to the hospital."

"Couldn't hurt."

"All right, so I'll do that. Thanks for working on this for me. Oh, and will you call Joy and let her know?"

"Of course. I'll talk to you later."

"Bye."

Anne hung up then slid out of the booth. Her feet were tired and her back ached, but she still had one more patient to walk to discharge before she was through. She turned and nearly bumped into someone standing next to the booth.

"Oh, I'm sorry—" she began, then cut off.

Staring at her, a squashed Styrofoam coffee cup in one hand, was a very angry Preston Winder.

Chapter Eighteen

COFFEE DRIBBLED FROM THE SQUASHED cup, over Preston's hand, to pool at his feet. If it burned, he didn't show it. Anne's focus turned to the whites of his eyes that were opened too wide and the muscles bunched in his clenched jaw.

"You *are* spying on me."

Anne's mouth went dry. "I…"

"Who are you working for? The lawyers?"

She swallowed and shook her head. "I'm a hospital volunteer."

"Don't give me that. Volunteers don't go around snooping into people's personal business." He threw the cup onto a table and snatched several napkins out of a dispenser. "What do you want? What are you trying to find?"

Anne drew a steadying breath. "Mr. Winder, you are correct. I *am* looking for something. One of the nurses here, Shirley Bashore, is my friend. Shirley was attacked last week, and I'm doing what I can to track down who did it."

She waited, but no flicker of defensiveness or fear crossed his features. He folded his arms and glared. "And? What does that have to do with—?"

He stopped, his mouth falling open. "Bashore. I know that name. She was one of the nurses who treated my son."

Was this an opportunity to draw him into a confession? Anne said a silent prayer for wisdom then gave a slow nod. "I know you blame the hospital for what happened."

"Of course I blame them," he spat, his hand slicing through the air. "I brought my son here thinking they would save his life. Instead they tied me up in legal paperwork."

"And now your wife has filed for a divorce. Do you blame the hospital for that too?"

His voice changed, became sad instead of bitter, and it cut Anne to the quick. "I sat in some office filling out insurance forms while my boy died. My wife never forgave me for not being there when he passed. So yes, Mrs. Mabry, I do blame the hospital for my divorce. It's just one more thing they've cost me." The anger returned, turning his lips white and the tips of his ears red. "And somehow, some way, I'm going to make sure they pay."

He whirled, and Anne let out a breath in a rush. Only now did she realize as she looked around the coffee shop that others had witnessed the scene between her and Preston. Two nurses still stared at her, and at the cash register, the barista looked as shocked as the customer who stood with his money clutched in his hand. Her phone rang, and Anne had never been so thankful to have an excuse to leave.

Stepping into a quiet corner of the lobby, she glanced at the screen then picked up. "Hey, Shirley."

"Hey, Anne. Good news. I got ahold of Susan. She *did* report Benny for doing some sloppy work and Benny *did* confront her about it. The day she was attacked, as a matter of fact."

"And the others?"

"I was only able to talk to Crystal. She said she's seen him be rude to people before but couldn't remember ever actually having words with him."

"And she never reported him or said anything to his supervisor?"

"Nope, but that doesn't mean there isn't another connection somewhere."

Maybe, but Anne wasn't convinced. She told Shirley about her second confrontation with Preston.

"I feel so sorry for him, Shirl. He's hurting and lashing out. I'm ashamed to say there were a few times I reacted exactly the same way after Ariane died."

Shirley listened quietly, and then said, "I can understand that, absolutely. Losing someone you love is hard enough. I can't even imagine the pain of losing a child. Still, grief doesn't give someone license to scare and harm innocent people."

Anne's eyes burned, but she managed to keep the tears at bay. "I'm going to finish up here and then run by the house to pick up some stuff for Lili. We'll talk more after I'm done, okay?"

"You know what? Why don't we just call it a day for now? This has been a lot, and we're both tired. Go home. Talk with Ralph. We'll think about everything else tomorrow."

Anne didn't argue. She hung up with Shirley then went upstairs to escort her last patient to discharge. Afterward, she ran by Lili's house and then dropped everything off at the hospital along with some food that Lili hadn't asked for but Anne knew she needed. By the time she finally made it home, she was weary to her bones and weighted with a deep, heavy mixture of remorse and concern.

"Bottom line, I don't want Preston to be guilty," she told Ralph later, as they sat in front of a cozy fire sipping their tea. "You and I know better than anyone what he's been through. What he's going through," she corrected. "I'm honestly praying he's not the person we're looking for."

Ralph chewed his lip thoughtfully, both elbows propped on the arms of his chair and his cup poised midway to his mouth. "It's been my experience that grief makes people do crazy things—things that might not have otherwise been in their nature to do."

Anne frowned. "So are you saying you think Preston might be guilty?"

Ralph's steady gaze met and held hers. "I'm saying it doesn't matter what we want. Our focus has to be on searching out the truth, regardless of who is guilty."

He was right, but it wasn't the answer Anne wanted. She sank deeper into her chair and finished the rest of her tea in silence. When it was gone, she rose and took her cup and Ralph's to the kitchen sink, then went back into the living room to kiss him good night.

"I'm gonna try to get some sleep," she said, laying her hand on her husband's strong shoulder. "Pray for me, will you?"

"I already am, honey," he said, taking her hand and pressing a kiss to her fingers. "I already am."

Chapter Nineteen

To Anne's surprise, she slept the entire night through and arrived at the hospital Thursday morning feeling better than she had in several days. Addie was being released later, so Anne popped in for a quick visit before heading downstairs to meet with Evelyn and Joy for a cup of coffee.

Sunlight streamed through the doors and windows of the lobby, casting the mums and pumpkins that decorated the entrance in a warm, orangey glow. Anne smiled. Maybe God was already answering her prayers and Ralph's. Maybe today they'd figure out who was behind the attacks and finally put the stress of it all behind them.

Evelyn was already in the back room of the gift shop when Anne got there, but the pot on the counter behind them was strangely empty.

"You two look like you're deep in conversation," she teased as she reached for the carafe to fill it with water. She turned to Joy. "Did you forget to set the timer?"

"I did. I was going to start it, but Shirley called before I had a chance," Joy said as she shot a glance at Evelyn.

"Shirley." Anne lowered the pot. "Well, I did talk to her yesterday about Preston. I figured she'd call you."

"It's not about Preston. Or, not about the case, anyway," Evelyn said. She looked at Joy.

Anne turned to rest her hip against the counter. "Okay, somebody better tell me what's going on. You two are making me nervous."

Evelyn motioned to a table and chairs. "We should sit down."

The feeling of foreboding in Anne's belly was growing worse by the minute. She pulled out a chair and sat without saying a word.

"Shirley is on her way," Evelyn said. "Garrison called her this morning and asked her to come in so they could talk about the litigation surrounding Preston's son."

"Apparently, her role in the whole affair has come under scrutiny," Joy said. She plucked a napkin from the dispenser and began tearing it to shreds. "Preston's lawyer called and was asking some very specific questions."

Anne's heart slammed into overdrive. "About Shirley?"

"That's what it sounded like," Evelyn said. "Shirley was pretty upset when she called, so we're not sure, but why else would Garrison ask her to come in?"

"I don't get it." Joy flung the napkin on the table and blew out an exasperated sigh. "Why in the world would his attorneys focus on Shirley? She's an excellent nurse."

"I think I know." Anne's hands began to shake. She clasped them tightly, her voice wobbling as she told them about the encounter with Preston. Both listened wide-eyed until she finished.

"Does Shirley know what happened?" Evelyn asked.

Anne nodded. "She called right after he left to tell me she'd talked to Susan and Crystal. Susan did report Benny, by the way, but Crystal didn't. No idea about the other two. We would have told y'all this sooner, but it was such a stressful day, we agreed not to think about it for the rest of the night. If I had known Preston would retaliate this way, I would have…"

What? Called them?

Anne could no longer hide the shaking of her clasped hands. Joy covered them with her own hands, and soon, Evelyn did the same.

"This is my fault," Anne whispered, meeting first Joy's gaze, and then Evelyn's. "All my snooping around has only made things worse for Shirley."

"We were all snooping, and we did it to help our friend," Evelyn replied.

"But I'm the one who insisted we do something. I'm the one who went by his house. If I had just let the police handle things instead of sticking my nose in where it didn't belong…"

"Then you would have been acting completely out of character," Evelyn said.

"We all would," Joy added. "We investigate. We try to help. It's what we do and how God made us."

Anne turned her head as movement near the door caught her eye. "Shirley." Anne jumped up from the table and hurried toward her. "I'm so sorry. Have you talked to Garrison?"

Shirley's brows rose. "Not yet, and what in the world do you have to be sorry about?"

Anne pinched her lips together, afraid if she said a word, she'd start crying.

Understanding creased Shirley's face. "Listen, Preston Winder is a hurting man looking for someone or something to pin his pain and anger on. It was only a matter of time until he turned his attention on me."

Anne dragged in a breath to help swallow the knot in her throat. "What time are you going up to see Garrison?"

Shirley glanced at her watch. "In about fifteen minutes. But I knew you all would be here. I figured we could come together and ask God for a bit of wisdom regarding what I should say to him."

"Of course," Joy said, drawing even with Anne.

Evelyn joined them on the other side. "Where two or more are gathered, right?"

"Right." Shirley looked at them all steadily before extending her hands. Forming a circle, they prayed for God's peace and strength, and then one by one, they asked a blessing over Shirley.

"Would you like someone to go with you, Shirley?" Joy asked, crossing closer to wrap her in a hug.

"That might not be a bad idea," she said. "I'll admit, it sure would be nice to have someone alongside me praying."

"I'll go," Anne volunteered quickly. "I don't have anything to do until after nine this morning. And besides…" She didn't finish and didn't have to. All three understood why she wanted to be there.

"We'll be praying for you both," Evelyn said, reaching out to squeeze Anne's arm. She directed a firm glance at Shirley. "But we expect you to let us know what he says as soon as it's over."

Shirley laughed and pulled Evelyn into a hug. "Of course we will. You two go on now. We'll meet up again in about an hour?"

She looked at Joy, who nodded. "Lacy is volunteering in the gift shop today. I'm sure it'll be no problem sneaking away for a few minutes."

Evelyn nodded too. With the Grove as the agreed-upon meeting place, the four of them parted.

The walk up to Garrison's office was quiet. Anne couldn't help but wonder what Shirley was thinking as they waited for Julie to let him know they'd arrived.

"You okay?" she whispered, glancing sidelong at her friend.

Shirley nodded, outwardly calm except for the slight twitching under her left eye.

"Mr. Baker is ready for you," Julie said, stepping back into the office.

Mr. Baker. Not Garrison? Anne stole a look at Shirley, but if she'd noted the change, she didn't let it show. Of course, this was hospital business, so it was appropriate for Julie to be more formal. Though he and Shirley were dating, today he had to be Mercy Hospital's administrator first.

Anne sucked in a breath as they entered Garrison's office. On the corner of his desk sat a fresh box of tissues. What exactly did he plan to say?

A host of what-ifs bombarded Anne's brain. What if Shirley lost her job? Or her license? What if Preston's attorney filed charges?

Anne pushed the questions away as Garrison met them halfway and walked them to his desk.

"Come on in, ladies. Please, have a seat." He laid his hands on the back of one chair, which Shirley took. Anne claimed the one next to it, and Garrison pulled up a third instead of sitting behind the desk.

He turned to Shirley and dove right in. "Okay, so obviously, I wanted to touch base with you before you talk to the attorneys."

She nodded.

"Anne," Garrison continued, "I gather you know what this is about since Shirley invited you to be here with her?"

"I do."

"And Shirley, you're okay with me talking about this in front of Anne?"

"Anything you have to say to me, you can say in front of her," Shirley replied, her voice far more calm than Anne felt. She lifted her chin and laced her hands in her lap. "I have nothing to hide."

"All right then." Garrison drew in a deep breath and met Shirley's gaze. "Preston's attorney is requesting information on every single step you took while assisting in the care of his son."

The news wasn't surprising.

"I've directed him to the statements you made a year ago, but he's pressing for copies of every note, every file, and every email— anything that could be in any way associated with his son."

"Why does he want those things?" Shirley asked. "What is he hoping he'll find?"

Garrison's lips thinned. "I suspect it's because he's hoping you will trip up and change your statement. Even small variations could be construed as evidence of a lie."

"All this took place over a year ago," Anne argued. "There's no possible way she could remember what she said down to that kind of detail."

"Just do the best you can," Garrison said.

Shirley leaned forward in her chair. "But you still seem worried."

He blew out a breath and nodded. "I am. Preston and his attorney have put a target on your back. There's no telling where this might lead." He reached across and took her hand. "I wanted you to be prepared…just in case."

His voice roughened at the end, showing how hard the words had been for him. Shirley must have noticed it too. Her eyes instantly filled with tears, and she turned her hand to grip his.

Anne stood. "I'm going to give you two a little time." She laid her hand on Shirley's shoulder. "If you need me, I'll be right outside."

Shirley didn't speak, or perhaps she couldn't. She nodded, and Anne eased out the door. At the desk, Julie shot her a sympathetic glance. Did she know what was going on? Probably.

Anne pointed to a chair farthest from the door. "Okay if sit for a minute?"

"Of course. Make yourself comfortable."

Comfortable wasn't perhaps the word to describe how she felt. Anne was upset. Angry. Afraid. Pretty much anything *but* comfortable. But she knew where those emotions came from and Who to turn to for relief. She closed her eyes.

God, please. Please take care of my friend. Please give her wisdom to know exactly what to say and stop her from saying anything that could be misconstrued or twisted. Lord, guide Garrison as he tries to protect both Shirley and the hospital. And…please show Preston that this isn't the way toward peace. Help him to find You, Lord. Help him to heal. Help him to forgive. Just…help. Please.

She opened her eyes, expecting to feel better. To feel peace, even though the situation hadn't changed. She expected to…but she didn't.

Why? God was able to do above and beyond anything she thought or asked. He could take care of Shirley. He could work things out with Preston.

Deep down, she started to sense what was bothering her. She knew He *could*. But what she feared, and what she couldn't bring herself to think…was whether He *would*.

And if He didn't, would she still praise Him?

Chapter Twenty

THE ANGEL OF MERCY STATUE stood sentinel over the south end of the Grove. Anne kept her gaze fixed to it as she and Shirley made their way down one of the tree-lined pathways to meet Joy and Evelyn. It had warmed up some outside, making the need for jackets unnecessary. Overhead, weak sunlight trickled through the leaves still clinging to the trees.

"Well?" Evelyn bounced from foot to foot as they approached. "How did it go?"

"What did Garrison say?" Joy added.

"Pretty much what we figured." Shirley dragged in a deep breath through her nose and blew it out through her mouth. "Let's sit and I'll tell y'all about it."

"So when do you meet with Preston's attorney?" Joy asked, scraping back one of the chairs that encircled the various bistro tables clustered around the Grove.

"And do you have to meet with him at all?" Evelyn asked, her eyebrows forming peaks that nearly reached her hairline. "For that matter, should you, without talking to a lawyer?"

"The hospital will send a legal representative with me," Shirley said. "I won't be by myself."

"I think what we're all wondering is whether or not you should get your own attorney," Anne said. "Especially if Preston's attorney is specifically out to get you."

Her throat thickened, making it hard to get the words out.

"This isn't your fault, Anne," Shirley said quietly.

She knew. Somehow, she knew what Anne was thinking. Anne blinked to stop the tears from forming and nodded.

Joy cleared her throat and lifted her hand to twist her hair around her finger. "Okay. For now, it's probably best if we put the questions about the muggings on hold. Does everyone agree on that?"

All three nodded.

Joy stood. "Good. Then what about tonight? It's Thursday, are we still going to work out?"

"I'm not sure I feel like it," Anne said.

"Me neither." Shirley shrugged. "I kinda just want to go home and sit in front of the TV. Maybe eat some ice cream. *Lots* of ice cream."

She laughed, but there was a quaver to her voice that sent a shot straight to Anne's heart. "It might be good for us to work off some steam," she said. "And a boost of adrenaline would be good for our mood. What do you say, Shirl?"

After a long moment, Shirley lifted her chin and nodded. "All right. I'll go home and check on Mama. Then I'll plan on meeting y'all back here around six."

"Good. That's good, Shirley." Evelyn clamped her mouth shut, but Anne had the sneaking suspicion it was because she was feeling a tad emotional too. Evelyn stood. "I'm off. I got a message from IT that my computer is ready. I'm gonna go pick it up. See you all this afternoon."

She whirled and headed off in the direction of the records department, but not before Anne spied the worry in her eyes.

"Okay, I'd better get back to the gift shop too." Joy turned. "Shirley, is there anything you need me to do before you head back this afternoon?"

"Not a thing. Thanks, though."

"Sure." She gave Shirley another hug, and then she was gone, leaving Anne and Shirley alone under the shadow of the Angel of Mercy statue.

For a long time, neither one spoke. Finally, Shirley's sigh broke the silence. "You know, I used to ask myself if there was anything I could have done differently. After Preston's son died, I mean. I wondered if he'd still be alive if I'd handled things differently."

She glanced at Anne, who nodded. "That's perfectly natural."

Shirley shrugged. "Maybe. But I've been doing it again since the attack. Thinking about Preston has dredged up some insecurity, made me reexamine my actions. In the heat of the moment, I know I did the best I could, but I'll probably always wonder...was it enough?" She shook her head.

"I'm praying for you, Shirley," Anne managed at last, forcing the words past a sudden lump in her throat.

"I know you are. I wouldn't expect anything less." Shirley stood and gave Anne a hug, then pulled a folded tissue out of her jacket pocket and pushed it into Anne's hand. "But you gotta stop blaming yourself for all of this, you hear? I've put myself in His hands. We need to trust that He's gonna take care of me. And He will. I just know it."

Anne wished she could be as certain. She smiled anyway and nodded. "Love you, Shirl. I'll see you tonight."

"Love you too."

Shirley waved and headed away from the hospital toward the parking garage. Anne watched her go a moment, then trudged inside. Normally, she loved her position as a volunteer at the hospital, but today she wanted nothing more than to rush into Ralph's arms and ask him to take her home.

Fortunately, she didn't have time to dwell on the thought. Between her own responsibilities and Polly's, Anne was busy all morning and late into the afternoon. Which was probably just as well, she told herself as she changed into her workout clothes. She'd worry herself into an ulcer otherwise.

Worry.

She frowned at the word. How many times had she talked to others about the uselessness of worry? She knew better and yet…she was afraid.

She drew up short at the startling admission. Not about the case. She trusted God with that. It was her loved ones she feared for…their vulnerability. And the fact that they could be taken away any moment. She sucked in a breath, her fingers tightening around the handle of her gym bag. She believed in God's love. Why, then, didn't she trust in His plan?

It was a painful revelation and a humbling one.

Sinking onto a bench between the rows of lockers, Anne closed her eyes and prayed first for God's forgiveness and then for the strength to trust Him with the people she cared about most. This time, when she opened her eyes, she did feel better. She walked down to the fitness studio with a smile on her lips.

Shirley was already there and so was Evelyn.

"Where's Joy?" Anne asked, slinging the long strap on her gym bag over her shoulder.

"On her way." Evelyn tapped her finger against her watch. "We're early. She said she was going to run home real quick and then meet us here."

"Okay. Should we go in?" Anne asked.

"Might as well." Shirley shrugged out of her jacket and draped it over her arm.

Inside the studio, low music played to an empty room.

"Wow. We really are early." Anne dropped her bag onto the floor, pulled open the zipper, and took out an empty water bottle. "I'm gonna fill this before class starts."

She headed toward the water fountain on the back wall of the studio. The hospital had recently installed touchless fountains, so Anne unscrewed the lid and stuck the bottle over the sensor to fill it. Behind her, the door to Talia's office opened. Expecting to see Talia, Anne was surprised when Marcus Seybold stepped through.

"Dr. Seybold, hello." Anne screwed the lid onto her water bottle and motioned toward the studio. "Are you joining our fitness class?"

"What?" His gaze followed where she pointed and then he shook his head. "Oh no. I'm not an aerobics class kinda guy. I prefer running. Just stopped in to check things out." Grabbing his lapels, he straightened his lab coat and flashed a smile, his teeth gleaming white against his tan. "Anyway, I should be going. Nice to see you again, Mrs. Mabry."

"You too, doctor. Have a good night."

He tipped his head in acknowledgment then ducked out the door.

"What was he doing here?" Evelyn asked, joining Anne at the water fountain.

"He said he was checking things out," Anne said, then shrugged. "He sure seemed in an awful hurry to leave."

Once again, the door next to them opened, and this time, it was Talia who walked out—straight past them and into the studio without saying a word.

Evelyn frowned. "Did she look upset to you?"

"A little." Anne leaned closer. "Her makeup was smudged like she'd been crying."

"Or it could have been sweat from the last workout," Evelyn suggested.

Maybe, but Anne wasn't convinced. "What do you suppose Dr. Seybold was doing in her office?"

"I hope he wasn't bothering her." Evelyn frowned.

He *was* known to be flirtatious with the hospital staff. But why would that have been upsetting to Talia? Unless she didn't welcome his advances and had told him so. But then, wouldn't he have been the one who looked upset?

"Come on." Evelyn snagged Anne's sleeve and tugged. "Class is about to start. I already grabbed you a mat."

Anne nodded and followed her onto the floor, where several people were already stretching.

"Where were you guys?" Joy whispered as they approached.

"We were talking about Dr. Seybold," Anne whispered back.

Joy's eyes widened, and she pointed to the floor. "He was here?"

"Yeah. He just left. Didn't you see him?"

Joy shook her head then licked her lips and looked around the room at the other people funneling in. "I heard a rumor today that he and Talia were kind of a thing."

"That would explain what he was doing here," Evelyn said.

And why his lab coat needed straightening. Except… "You said they *were* a thing?"

Joy nodded. "Lacy said Talia broke it off a couple of weeks ago, but Dr. Seybold has been pretty persistent in trying to win her back. She said Talia told her he isn't the type to take no for an answer. Lacy said she even looked nervous when she said it."

"Nervous, how?" Anne asked.

Joy shrugged. "I probably should have asked, but I didn't."

Anne pondered this as they warmed up for class. Talia's instincts about Benny had been spot on. Could it be she had a reason to be nervous about Dr. Seybold too?

Grabbing her mat, Anne circled around Evelyn and Joy and dropped it next to Shirley, who was folded in half, touching her toes. Anne matched her pose.

"How well do you know Dr. Seybold?" she asked, lowering her voice so the people around them couldn't hear.

Shirley let go of her toes and looked sideways at Anne. "I've worked with him on a couple of different cases. Why?"

"Would you say he's persistent?"

She huffed and pressed her palms to the floor. "Stubborn is more like it. Some would say arrogant. I'll just say the man likes to get his way." She blew out a breath and straightened then propped her hands on her hips. "What's this about? Why the questions about Dr. Seybold?"

She asked a tad too loud. Several people closest to them glanced in their direction, including Talia.

Anne angled her head toward the front of the class. "We'd better pay attention."

Following the direction she indicated, Shirley sucked in a breath as she turned her gaze to her mat. For the rest of class, they didn't speak, just concentrated on doing the moves Talia led them through, although Anne wasn't all that surprised when she approached them afterward.

"Anne, have you got a minute?" Her face was flushed. Around her neck, she clutched a towel by both ends. Tightly. So tightly, she turned the skin over her knuckles white.

Anne turned to Shirley, Evelyn, and Joy. "I'll catch up with you gals in a second."

"We'll be in the coffee shop," Joy said, then looked at Talia. "Great class today, Talia. Thank you."

"No problem. Thanks for coming." Though she was polite, her impatience showed in the tapping of her toe.

Anne waited until Joy left before clearing her throat. "Listen, Talia, if this is about Dr. Seybold—"

"It is, but not how you think," she interrupted. She gestured toward the back of the studio and her office. "Do you mind?"

"Not at all. Just let me grab my bag." When she'd fetched it from the floor where she'd dropped it, Anne turned and followed Talia to the office. Once inside, Talia dragged the towel off her neck and used it to wipe her face.

"I take it you saw Dr. Seybold leaving here this afternoon?"

"I did." Anne waited, curious as to what Talia had to say.

"And you know about the rumors regarding him and me." It wasn't a question. Talia met her gaze resolutely.

Anne looked steadily back. "I didn't, until tonight. Talia, what is this about? Why did you want to speak to me?"

Sighing, Talia crossed to a cloth bin and dropped the towel inside. Afterward, she braced both hands on the metal handles and looked up at Anne. "Did you know that Dr. Seybold was married?"

"I…knew he was once."

"His wife divorced him a few years ago because she said she couldn't trust him. But she still loves him." She watched Anne a second then let go of the bin and stood upright. "How do I know that? Because she came to me a couple of weeks ago. Told me she wanted to reconcile with him. Asked me to stop seeing him." She shook her head. "No, she didn't ask. She threatened. Said if I didn't stop seeing him, she'd go to the hospital administration and have me fired."

Yes, that qualified as a threat. Anne licked her lips nervously. "Forgive me, but I'm still not sure what any of this has to do with me."

"I told Elaine Seybold that I wouldn't see Marcus anymore. If she hears that he came to see me, or if she thinks that I encouraged him…" She left off, and her gaze turned pleading. "I heard you talking to your friend about Dr. Seybold."

"Yes. I asked her how well she knew him."

"And?"

"She said she's worked with him a time or two."

Talia nodded quickly. "Anne, do you think you or your friend could talk to Marcus? Maybe convince him to stay away? I've tried, but he won't listen."

"Oh…I'm not sure…"

"I wouldn't ask if I wasn't desperate. I need this job, but I can't risk Elaine making good on her threat."

"If that's true, then maybe you should file a complaint with HR," Anne said.

"That's just it—I can't. I don't know who Elaine knows, and I can't risk telling the wrong person about Marcus's advances."

"Talia, what you're describing is harassment," Anne said. "I'm not the right person to handle something like that."

"No, no, I realize you're not. I just thought… Well, you seemed so friendly last time we talked, and I wondered if maybe…" She stumbled to a stop and held up both hands. "You're right. I shouldn't have asked. I'm sorry."

"I could put you in touch with someone in Human Resources," Anne began, but Talia backed up a step and shook her head.

"No. Thank you, but no. I'll just have to figure out something else on my own."

"What about talking to my husband?" Anne pressed. "He's the chaplain here at Mercy. Maybe he could advise you on some steps you could take, help you with setting boundaries, that sort of thing."

"I'd talk to him if I thought it would help," Talia said, her shoulders sagging. "The problem is, if Elaine is half as ruthless as her husband…"

Anne narrowed her eyes. "What do you mean 'ruthless'?"

She shrugged. "Marcus is very handsome and charming at first. But once you get past that, he can be very determined."

"As in, someone who won't take no for an answer?" Which was the same thing she'd told Lacy.

"Exactly." She hugged her arms around herself, her bottom lip trembling. "I thought I knew him. The truth is, I have no idea to what sort of lengths he'll go to get what he wants."

Caught off guard, Anne held up her hands. "Wait, are you saying you're afraid of Marcus?"

"Not just Marcus. His ex-wife. I wish I'd never met them. I'm sorry. It's just, I don't know that many people here, and I wasn't sure who to ask." She dropped her arms and then, as though she could no longer hold back the flood, Talia burst into tears.

"Um…"

In the span of a second, compassion flooded over Anne. It was true that Talia didn't know many people at the hospital. It was also apparently true that she needed this job very much. Both of those facts compelled Anne to help her.

The question was…how?

Chapter Twenty-One

THE DOOR TO DR. SEYBOLD's office was ajar when Anne got there Friday morning, but no one was inside. Anne hesitated to go in, except that Marilyn's computer was on, and steam rose from a cup near the keyboard, as though she'd just stepped away and would be back any moment. Choosing a chair near the door, Anne sat down to wait. It wasn't long before Dr. Seybold strode in, dressed in scrubs, his lab coat draped over his arm.

"Oh. Mrs. Mabry. Is Marilyn not—?" He looked around, his brow crumpling in a displeased frown. "I'm so sorry. Marilyn appears to be gone. Again." He dropped the lab coat over the back of her chair then crossed his arms. "Is there something I can help you with?"

Here it was. The moment of truth. Why, oh why, had she agreed to help Talia with something that was none of her concern?

Anne cleared her throat and clutched the handles on her purse. "Actually, I was hoping to see you, that is, if you have a moment?"

His gaze fell to the calendar on Marilyn's desk. "Did we have an appointment? If Marilyn forgot to write it down—"

"No, no, we didn't. Should I have called first?"

"Under normal circumstances, I would say no. Unfortunately, I'm due in surgery soon." He looked at a clock on the wall above a bank of filing cabinets then let out an exaggerated sigh. "Oh, for heaven's sake. Would you excuse me a second?"

He held up one finger, then half turned and brought his smart watch to his mouth. "Marilyn, where are you? I need you back at the office. Now." Lowering his wrist, he looked sheepishly at Anne. "Sorry about that."

"No problem." She tucked her hair behind her ear and stood. "I should probably be going anyway."

"Oh, well...all right..." He floundered a moment then gestured toward her. "Listen, if you'd like to leave your number..." He fumbled through the things on Marilyn's desk, muttering about the lack of paper and pen. Finally, he gave up and motioned to the empty chair. "If you don't mind waiting, you can leave your number with her when she gets back. I'll call you when I get out of surgery."

Dr. Seybold was obviously unhappy with Marilyn at the moment. It was awkward and uncomfortable, but it reminded Anne of Marilyn's complaint about not being promoted.

"Yes, I'll wait. Thank you, Dr. Seybold."

He nodded then marched out the door. Left at loose ends, Anne wandered around the office. There were pictures on the walls, but none were of Marilyn or her family. Most were framed medical posters, but here and there were images of Dr. Seybold—one on a fishing trip with friends she didn't recognize and another of him on a beach holding a tropical-looking drink.

Marilyn burst through the door. "Dr. Seybold—oh." Huffing, she wiped a trail of sweat from her temple as she made her way to the desk. In her hand was a boxed salad, which she stored in a small refrigerator behind her desk. "Sorry. The delivery guy was lost. I had to go and meet him."

"No problem."

Marilyn yanked open her desk drawer and took out a tissue that she used to dab the sweat from her face. "You needed to see me?"

"No, I came to see Dr. Seybold, but he was on his way to surgery. He asked me to leave a number." She motioned to the desk.

"Okay." Marilyn pulled her chair away from the desk, scowling as she took Dr. Seybold's lab coat and tossed it on top of the filing cabinets.

"Another lab coat." Anne smiled.

Marilyn didn't smile back. She stared at Anne, one hand still on the chair. "Huh?"

Anne pointed to the filing cabinets. "You were looking for a lab coat last time I was here. Did you find it?"

"Oh." Marilyn shook her head and sat. "No, I didn't. Not surprising though. The man plays off the whole 'doctor' persona." She crooked two fingers in the sign of air quotes then rolled her eyes. "He keeps one to wear outside the hospital. Can't believe some women still fall for that."

It appeared the entire day was destined to be filled with awkward conversations. Anne bit back a grimace and gestured to the pictures on the wall in an attempt to lighten the mood. "That's a nice picture of Dr. Seybold. Is it recent?"

Marilyn looked where she pointed and nodded. "From his last vacation."

Anne smiled. "Sure would be nice to be on a beach somewhere right now, what with the weather turning colder. Was that taken around here?"

"Bahamas." She took out a pen and a notebook and laid them on the desk. "If you'd like to leave your number?"

So no chitchat for Marilyn today. Anne swallowed and reached for the pen, while Marilyn picked up her cup and carried it to a small microwave next to the refrigerator. While she warmed her coffee, Anne jotted down her name and cell phone number. Bending near the desk also gave her a clear look at Marilyn's desk calendar and its rows of highlighted dates. In one color, the same note and time were repeated over and over—*Run 8:15 P.M.*

Run? Dr. Seybold liked to run. He'd said so when Anne asked if he was joining their fitness class. So the highlighted times weren't patient appointments?

"Ahem." Marilyn startled Anne by returning to the desk and sliding the desk calendar away. "All set?"

"Sorry. Yes." Anne returned the paper and pen, then waved at the calendar. "I couldn't help but notice that Dr. Seybold runs every day."

"He likes to keep fit." Marilyn snorted. "Of course, it's no secret why. He has a penchant for pretty young women. Even his wife knew."

There was a note of defensiveness in her voice as she added the last, as though she were trying to justify talking poorly about her boss.

"Do you know Elaine Seybold?" Anne asked, steering the conversation away from the rumors regarding Dr. Seybold.

"I've met her a couple of times," Marilyn replied, letting each word roll slowly off her tongue, as though choosing them with care. "I know people say she can be a little haughty, but if you ask me, she's a saint for putting up with as much as she did. Still, even saintly women can be pushed too far, if you know what I mean."

She didn't know, and she hadn't asked, but there was no doubting the implied innuendo. Did Marilyn know more than she was saying, or was this an attempt to cast suspicion on someone else? And how would she find out?

"Well, I should get going," Anne said, nodding at the clock. "I have to be at the volunteer office in a few minutes. Thanks for chatting with me, and if you wouldn't mind giving my number to Dr. Seybold?"

"Of course." Marilyn ripped the page out of the notebook then reached for the tape dispenser. "I'll see that he gets it."

"Thank you."

Anne let herself out of the office. She hadn't finished what she came for, but she couldn't help feeling that maybe she'd accomplished something else. As she headed toward the volunteer office, she wracked her brain for someone who might be able to tell her a little more about Elaine Seybold. Joy was a possibility since she attended a lot of social functions at the hospital. And then it hit her. Shirley, of course. She said she'd worked with Dr. Seybold before. Maybe she knew something about his wife.

She looked at her watch. Any questions regarding Elaine would have to wait if she wanted to avoid being late. Aurora had already posted changes to the day's assignments on the bulletin board, so Anne grabbed hers and hurried off to meet her first patient. While she did her best to show attention and care to the people she helped, Preston and Marilyn weighed heavily on her mind, as did Marilyn's insinuation that Elaine Seybold had been pushed too far. But how was that tied to the muggings?

Unless...

People said Dr. Seybold liked to flirt. And Talia had said that Elaine was jealous and wanted to reconcile with her ex-husband. Could jealousy be the connection? Maybe Dr. Seybold had come on to the victims, and Elaine had retaliated by trying to get them out of the picture.

Anne shook her head. It was too far of a stretch. Still, she could ask Shirley about the possibility just to scratch Elaine off the suspect list.

The scenarios ran endlessly through Anne's head while she counted the minutes until her first break. Finally, it came, and Anne hurried to a quiet corner of the Grove to make the call to Shirley. When she answered, Anne peppered her with questions.

"Shirley, it's Anne. Didn't you tell me last night that you'd worked with Dr. Seybold? What was he like? Did he ever try to flirt with you? And have you ever met his wife?"

"Whoa, whoa. Hold on there. What's this about?"

Drawing a breath, Anne backed up and told Shirley about her conversation with Talia and subsequent visit to see Dr. Seybold. "Marilyn made it sound like Elaine had cause to be vindictive, but I'm not so sure," Anne finished. "I kinda got the feeling she was trying to throw me off track. Still, I figured I'd better check all my bases."

"So that's why you asked if he'd ever tried to flirt with me?"

"Uh-huh."

"Well." Shirley's voice took on a sharp edge. "He's never flirted with me, but then again I doubt he would since we tend to butt heads a bit. He doesn't like having his authority questioned."

Her comment drew Anne up short. "What do you mean?"

"His patient notes. I questioned him on something he wrote in a medical report and heard all about it the next day. Apparently, he thought I'd overstepped and told me in no uncertain terms that he didn't appreciate it."

This was news Anne hadn't expected. She paused, thinking over what she'd learned about Dr. Seybold and his habit of running in the evenings. "Shirley, do you know if the other victims have had similar experiences with Dr. Seybold?"

"I'm not so sure about the other victims, but Susan for sure has. In fact, I don't think there are too many nurses here that haven't gotten crossways with him."

"And when that happens, how many of them report it to HR?"

"A few, I guess. You'd probably have to ask…"

"Crystal," they said in unison.

"Yeah." Shirley sucked in a breath. "Anne, do you think maybe we've been looking at this situation wrong this whole time?"

"I don't know. Maybe." A brisk wind had kicked up, scattering a pile of leaves and sending them skittering along the pavement. Anne squeezed the phone to her ear and rubbed her hand over her arm. "I've gotta get back to work soon. Do you think you could check with Crystal on the complaints, and maybe see what you can find out about the former Mrs. Seybold?"

"I'll do what I can."

"Thanks, Shirley."

Anne disconnected and then scurried toward the gift shop to fill Joy in on everything they'd learned. To her surprise, Joy was hurrying out the door just as she arrived.

"Anne, there you are." Nearly bouncing with excitement, Joy grabbed her by the arm. "I just got off the phone with Evelyn. Did she tell you? There's been a breakthrough in the case. I know we've been suspicious of Preston this whole time, but I think we've been looking at this thing all wrong."

Anne blinked in confusion. How could Joy have heard about Dr. Seybold already?

"I don't think Preston's our culprit," Joy continued.

Anne started to open her mouth, but Joy's next statement cut the words from her mouth.

"Our intuition about Benny was right. Benny is our mugger!"

Chapter Twenty-Two

"Hold on, now." Anne pressed the fingertips of both hands to her temples, where a small ache had begun to thrum. "What do you mean, Benny is our mugger? He can't be. I just figured out it might be Dr. Seybold."

"Really?" Joy drew her head back and frowned. "What are you talking about?"

"What are *you* talking about?"

Joy made a visible action of clearing her thoughts with a shake of her head. "Evelyn called and said she'd heard the mugger might have been injured in the last attack."

"What?"

Joy nodded. "Apparently, Susan has been taking some self-defense classes and used her keys to fend off the attacker. According to Susan, she may have managed to cut their hand and possibly tear the person's shirt."

Still confused, Anne scratched her head. "But why haven't we heard anything about this before now?"

"The police and security wanted to keep it quiet, not let the attacker know that there'd been a possible breakthrough."

"And now?"

"Now they're asking for the public's help. They put out a press release asking for any information that could tie possible suspects to the case. But that's not all." Once again, Joy gripped Anne by the arm. "Benny was spotted this morning with a bandage on his hand. It can't be coincidental, can it? Not with his history."

Anne blew out a breath. No wonder Joy was so sure he was guilty. "Have the police questioned him?"

"Not formally—as in bringing him down to the station. They did talk to him though. The rumor is that Benny told the police he got hurt at work."

"And they believed him?"

Joy shrugged. "I guess so. They would have taken him for questioning otherwise, right?"

"Good night, nurse." Anne rubbed her chin, thinking. "I wish we could get a look at Benny's hand. Even though I'm not certain it would tell us anything, I'd sure love to get a look at the cut."

"We could." Joy pointed toward the ceiling. "He's working upstairs now. Fourth floor."

"Hmph. I just came from there."

"Right." Joy snapped her fingers. "I was so excited about Benny, I forgot you were talking about something else. So what were you saying about Dr. Seybold being our culprit?"

Anne filled her in, ending with the highlighted dates she'd seen on Marilyn's calendar, and what she'd told her about his running habits.

"I admit, the time is a little suspicious," Joy said when she'd finished.

Joy stumbled forward as someone bumped her from behind.

"Oh, I'm so sorry." A woman in a large coat and sunglasses reached out as though to steady her. "Please excuse me. I should've been watching where I was going."

"No problem." Joy smiled. "Can we help you find something?"

"I'm looking for the gift shop."

"It's back that way." Joy pointed. "I'll be happy to help you in just a moment."

"No rush. Thank you so much." The woman gave a quick wave and bustled off.

"As I was saying," Anne continued, "I thought the time seemed a little too coincidental too, which is why I came looking for you."

After a second, Joy covered her mouth with her hand and nodded. "So? What are we going to do?"

"Right now, Shirley is checking on Crystal, plus seeing what she can find out about the ex-Mrs. Seybold."

"Okay. And what about us? What should we be doing?"

"Well, I *thought* I was going to talk to Dr. Seybold. Now, I think it's more important that I see what I can find out about Benny's injury."

"Okay." Joy bunched both fists in excitement. "Let me know what you learn. I gotta get back to work."

Anne nodded and then Joy spun and hustled toward the gift shop. Anne threw a glance heavenward. Just when she thought they'd made headway, this came out of left field. Still, if she wanted to talk to Benny, there was no time like the present.

Crossing to the elevators, Anne pondered how best to ask Benny about his hand. She'd always found being forthright to be fruitful, but was she asking for trouble if he had something to hide?

A good man out of the good treasure of his heart bringeth forth that which is good; and an evil man out of the evil treasure of his heart bringeth forth that which is evil: for of the abundance of the heart his mouth speaketh.

The verse from Luke popped into her head. She'd memorized it long ago, and hoped the truth of it would play out now.

Outside of the restrooms, Anne spotted Benny. With the bandage on his hand, he appeared to be struggling to knot the top of a trash bag. She hurried forward to help.

"Can I do that for you?"

Benny eyed her volunteer smock and arched a brow at her. "I can get it. Thanks anyway."

Anne nodded and motioned to his hand. "It must be hard to do your job with that bandage you're wearing. Did it happen at work?"

His gaze narrowed. He dropped the trash bag into a large bin on his custodial cart, then crossed his arms. "Yeah."

But he didn't say how. Interesting. "A worker's comp injury? Have you told your supervisor?"

His lips thinned. "What is this? You're not from HR. Did they send you to check up on me?"

Was his defensiveness due to distrust of a stranger, or something else? She lifted her hands. "What would make you think HR sent me?"

"Right." He bobbed his head knowingly then jabbed his finger at her. "Listen, I checked with my lawyer. That time I served? Those charges were bogus and it's getting expunged. That means I'm under no obligation to report it to my employer, so you can march right back to HR or whoever you work for and tell them I said so, okay?"

Not waiting for an answer, he stormed off, the custodial cart rattling behind him.

Anne bit the inside of her cheek in consternation. Benny hadn't answered when she asked if he'd reported the injury to his supervisor, but it would be easy enough to find out. She even had time before she needed to check in with the departments.

Her mind made up, Anne hurried down to the first floor in search of the custodial manager. On the office door, the name Earl Sheffield was engraved on a gold plaque. Anne knocked and let herself in.

The custodial manager's office was much like the oldest part of the records room—windowless and dusty, with unadorned red brick walls and a bare floor. A rusted beige filing cabinet dominated one corner, and across from it, an artificial ficus tree in a wicker planter collected cobwebs.

Anne didn't miss the irony of it.

Rustling noises from a room off the main office caught Anne's attention. She craned her neck to see around the corner. Spotting no one, she cleared her throat and called out, "Hello?"

An older woman with mousy brown hair and wearing a gray cable knit sweater popped into view. "Oh, hello. Sorry, I didn't hear you come in."

She shuffled toward Anne, holding a mug in one hand and the string on a teabag with the other. The scent of apples and cinnamon floated from the mug. It was the only pleasant odor in a room full of conflicting smells—like bleach and...was that mothballs?

"What can I do for you?"

Anne pointed to the name on the door. "I'm looking for Earl Sheffield?"

She shook her head. "Sorry, hon, Mr. Sheffield's off today. Is there something I can help you with?"

"Actually, I just had a couple of questions for him about one of his employees. Benny Pierce?" Anne dug a pen out of her smock pocket, held it up, and pretended to write. "Do you think I could leave him a message to call me?"

"Sure, that'd be fine." She set the mug down and dug through the piles on her desk for a notepad. When she found one, she pushed it to Anne. "Here you go."

Catching sight of the inside of the mug, Anne blinked. While it smelled heavenly, the milk had definitely curdled and floated in small white flecks atop the tea.

While Anne wrote, the woman brought the mug to her lips and took a sip. "Sure is nice to have a visitor. Hardly anyone comes down here anymore. Now it's all this." She picked up a radio and gave it a wiggle. "That or cell phones. Can you believe there's an app that does the same thing as a walkie-talkie?"

Anne smiled then tore off the paper and handed it to her. "Here you go. Thank you so much."

She studied what Anne had written and nodded. "Mabry, huh? You related to the chaplain?"

"Yes, as a matter of fact. He's my husband." Anne's smile widened. "Do you know Ralph?"

She grabbed the string on the teabag and gave it a swirl. "Not personally, but I've heard good things about him. People say he's a very good listener. Makes me glad to have him on board."

"Well, thank you, um…" Anne frowned. "Sorry, I don't think I caught your name."

"Nora."

"Yes. Thank you, Nora."

"No problem. Come visit anytime. You enjoy the rest of your day, now."

"You too."

Anne waved and then let herself out the way she'd come in. She shot a quick text to Joy, but figuring it would take too long to explain everything that had happened, asked if she wanted to meet up for dinner instead, since Ralph was sitting with Addie while Lili went to class, and Anne would be eating alone. She immediately responded with a yes and offered to contact Shirley and Evelyn.

The plan set, Anne went about the rest of her duties. By quitting time, she was tired and hungry and more than eager to hash things over with her friends. Maybe one of them could offer insight she'd missed in her conversations with Marilyn and Benny.

The agreed-upon meeting place was a restaurant near the water named Pete's. Famous for its shrimp and grits, subdued decor, and live music, it was one of Anne's favorite places to go with Ralph when they wanted a romantic night out. This evening, however, romance was the furthest thing from her mind.

Since she was the last to arrive, she hurried to join the others and was glad they'd chosen a table tucked into a quiet corner, because the place was already starting to fill. Along with the chatter of the customers, the clink of dishes and low music filled the air, making it hard to hear.

"I ordered tea for you," Joy said, sliding a glass and a bowl of lemon wedges toward her. "Hope that was okay."

"Perfect." Anne unwrapped a straw, stuck it in the glass, and took a sip then slid the strap of her purse over the back of her chair. "What a day."

"So? What happened with Benny?" Joy asked.

"You talked to Benny?" Evelyn twisted her antique engagement ring on her finger.

Anne nodded. "Joy told you about the bandage?"

Both Evelyn and Shirley nodded. Anne spilled the details, and then told them she'd asked his boss to call. "Hopefully I'll hear from him in the morning," she finished, reaching for a lemon wedge to squeeze into her tea.

The waitress appeared, and the women gave their order before proceeding.

"So, back to the case." Anne glanced at Shirley. "Were you able to get ahold of Crystal?"

Shirley nodded. "Yeah, but she wouldn't share much. Complaints filed by staff are confidential. I still found it interesting that she wouldn't say there *were* no complaints against Dr. Seybold." She lifted her eyebrows and glanced at them. "Does that mean something, or am I reading too much into it?"

Evelyn pushed a lock of silver hair behind her ear. "Hard to say. That's really not much to go on."

"What about Elaine Seybold?" Anne asked. "Did you find out anything about her?"

Shirley leaned forward and laced her slender fingers on the tabletop eagerly. "I did, and it's Elaine Gilbert now. She's using her maiden name." She went on to tell them everything she'd learned—from Elaine's family history, to college friends, and a list of the places she'd worked.

"Which, now that I listen to it"—she glanced around the table at them—"doesn't sound like much of anything that can help." She slumped into her chair. "Sorry, girls."

"It does help," Anne insisted. "You didn't share anything incriminating because there was nothing there to find."

"Which makes Marilyn sound like she may have been trying to direct suspicion somewhere besides herself," Evelyn said, nodding to Anne. "You may have been right about her."

"Maybe. Though this does make me wonder why Talia said what she did about her." Anne sighed. "I just wish I didn't feel like all we've done is work ourselves back to square one. Eventually, we have to stumble onto something helpful, right?"

Shirley's phone rang, and she dug into her purse to pull it out. Her eyes rounded as she read the name on the screen. "It's Garrison."

The phone rang a second time, then a third, and still Shirley didn't answer.

"Maybe it's good news," Anne said.

"Or maybe he just wants to talk to you, see how you're doing," Joy added.

Shirley nodded hesitantly and picked up. Besides her greeting, she said nothing for a long while. Watching her face, Anne's feeling of dread grew. Finally, Shirley nodded.

"I understand. Thanks for calling, Garrison. And thank you for your encouragement. Goodbye."

Anne held her breath, almost afraid to ask, but the desire to know more would not go away. "So? What did he have to say?"

Shirley didn't look at them as she put her phone into her purse, fidgeted with the strap, and then pulled the zipper closed. At last, she lifted her head. "Well...it wasn't good news," she said.

Chapter Twenty-Three

ANNE DROVE HOME IN A haze, the burden of everything Shirley had said crashing over her in waves—relentless and suffocating. A light still glowed from the kitchen, so Anne made her way there first. Ralph sat at the table, a cup of hot chocolate at his elbow, his glasses perched on his nose and the evening paper opened to the crossword puzzle spread out before him.

He looked up as she dropped her keys on the counter. "Hey, sweetheart. Long day?"

"That's one way to put it." Anne crossed to the table and plopped into the chair next to Ralph's. "How'd it go with Addie?"

"Actually, she's here." He jabbed his thumb toward the living room. "Lili stayed late at the library trying to catch up on the assignments she missed while Addie was in the hospital. She hasn't had a chance to buy groceries, so I brought Addie over here. I made her supper and some hot chocolate, and then she fell asleep on the couch. Want me to get you some? There's plenty on the stove."

"In a minute." She pecked a kiss on Ralph's cheek then tiptoed to the living room to check on Addie. Across the room, happy music from a children's program droned. Anne grabbed the remote and shut it off. As Ralph said, the girl slept soundly, her mouth opened just enough to let a soft snore slip past her lips. At her feet, the blanket had pooled. Anne grabbed a corner of it and dragged it up over her shoulders then sank onto the floor next to the couch.

She missed these times. Though she was glad to have Lili home, she longed for the days of tucking Addie into bed and reading her stories until she fell asleep.

Rising onto her knees, Anne whispered a prayer for sweet dreams as she placed a light kiss on Addie's honey-scented hair. Looking at her softly rounded cheeks, flushed with color from sleep, and the curls clinging to her forehead, Anne found it hard to believe she'd been so sick just a few days ago.

"Thank You for watching over her," Anne said, smoothing a few loose strands from Addie's face. "And thank You that she's here with us now."

She watched Addie silently a few seconds longer before she rose to rejoin Ralph in the kitchen. A second cup of hot chocolate sat on the table next to his. Anne reached for it and took a long sip. It was decadent and rich, with just the faintest hint of peppermint to heighten her senses.

"Mmm."

Ralph smiled. "Good?"

"Too good." Anne set down her cup and reclaimed the chair she'd left. After grabbing the pencil Ralph had been using to do the crossword, she began drawing circles on one corner of the paper, round and round, darker and darker, until she'd almost pressed through.

Ralph's hand closed over hers. "All right. Spill. What happened tonight?"

She looked at him in surprise. "Huh?"

He tipped his head toward the paper. "You're doodling. What's on your mind?"

Heaving a sigh, Anne set down the pencil and told him about Benny, and Marilyn, and Preston, and Dr. Seybold.

"That's interesting," he said, when she stopped long enough to draw a breath. His eyes narrowed, and he took hold of her hand and pressed a kiss to her fingers. "But what's really bothering you?"

Anne let her shoulders droop. Ralph could always tell when something was wrong. "It's Shirley," she said at last. "Garrison called to tell her that the hospital attorney is questioning some of the steps she took the night Preston's son died."

Ralph's eyes widened. "The *hospital* attorney? Not Preston's?"

Anne nodded and pulled her hand away. "Garrison kept saying it wasn't indicative that they thought she did anything wrong, but Shirley said she could tell he was worried. Why would the attorney ask these questions if everything was fine?"

"I can understand his concern."

"I feel so bad, Ralph." Anne planted both elbows on the table and ran her fingers through her hair. "If I hadn't drawn Preston's attention, he might never have asked his attorney to look into Shirley."

Ralph laced his fingers around his cup. "Now, Anne, think about what you're saying. Would Shirley want you to feel like you had to cover something up for her?"

"No." She fell silent a moment, hunching over to lean onto her crossed arms, then said, "I just feel so sorry for her, Ralph. She told me that the last few months she's gone over and over her actions from that night, wondering if Preston's son would still be alive if she'd done something different."

He pushed his cup aside and shook his head. "What-ifs are never helpful, and they tend to lead to discouragement and self-doubt."

"You're right about that. This new questioning is causing Shirley to doubt herself a little."

"I'm sorry about that, but it's pretty understandable too. Thinking about what she said, what she did…it's bound to make her relive the challenges she faced handling a life-or-death situation." Ralph took her hand. "Why don't we pray for her now?"

Anne nodded, peace washing over her as she listened to her husband pray. When he finished, she squeezed his fingers.

"Thank you, sweetheart. I told Shirley we would be praying for her."

"And we'll continue to do that until all of this with Shirley and the muggings at the hospital get resolved."

He said it with so much confidence, it took her back. "How do you know they will be?" she asked, mouth dry and throat tight.

"Well, I trust God's faithfulness, for one thing."

She dropped her gaze. Ralph tucked his finger under her chin and lifted it up again.

"Even if it's not the answer we want, it will be the answer that's best." He smiled a sweet, crooked half grin that stole her breath. He leaned closer until their foreheads almost touched and dropped his voice to a whisper. "Besides, if I know my wife, and I'm pretty sure I do, you are way too stubborn to give up until you've figured all this out."

Anne chuckled, low at first, then louder and harder until they were both laughing.

"Ralph Mabry," she managed between gasping breaths, "you know me too well."

"Hey, what's going on in here?"

Anne stopped laughing and jerked around to see Addie standing in the entrance. With her hair all tousled, and her eyes droopy with sleep, she looked like the cherubs on all the Christmas postcards Anne had ever seen.

"I'm sorry, sweetheart," she said, getting up to wrap her granddaughter in a gentle hug—one that felt much higher than it used to. How was it possible that Addie reached almost to Anne's shoulder? She cupped her chin and smiled down at her granddaughter. "Did we wake you?"

"Uh-huh, but that's okay. I like hearing you and Grandpa laugh." Addie's lips parted in a funny, gap-toothed grin that melted Anne's heart.

Ralph joined them and bent so that he was eye level with Addie. "Oh yeah? Well, just you wait until you're all healed up. You've got a whole lot of tickles coming, and then we'll see who's laughing."

Addie giggled but stopped when the glow of headlights flashed across the wall.

"Mom's home!"

Home. It warmed Anne's heart to know she still thought of it that way. Of course, in her eyes, it would always be Addie's home. Lili's too. She crossed to the kitchen door and flipped on the porch light. Lili entered a moment later, circles under her eyes but a smile for Addie on her face.

She hugged Ralph, then Anne, and then bent to kiss her daughter's cheek. "Hey, sweetheart. I thought you'd be asleep by now. You ready to go home?"

Anne couldn't help but feel a touch deflated by the question. Ralph seemed to sense her mood and slipped his arm around her waist. She smiled up at him, then motioned to the living room. "I'll go get Addie's things."

"Thanks, Mom."

Anne heard Lili and Ralph talking while she stuffed Addie's teddy bear into a brightly colored unicorn backpack. Her blanket had slipped to the floor. Anne pressed it to her nose and took a deep whiff. It smelled like warm honey...like Addie. Smiling, she picked up her shoes and carried everything back into the kitchen and set it all next to the door.

"Thanks again for watching her, Dad," Lili was saying as she helped Addie into her coat. "I didn't think I was ever going to get caught up on my homework, but I managed to get quite a bit done tonight."

"I'm glad to do it, sweetheart. Anytime." He chucked Addie under the chin then gave both her and Lili a big hug. "You grab her bag," he said to Lili. "I'll carry this little pumpkin out to the car."

"Okay." Lili circled to Anne and gave her one last hug before following Ralph out to the car.

Anne watched them go, her mouth clamped shut to keep a tidal wave of worry from washing out.

Get some rest. You look tired.

Put Addie's shoes on so her feet don't get cold.

Drive safe, and don't forget to buckle up.

These were all good things. Loving things. But Anne had learned over time that they made Lili feel like she was meddling.

"Trust God's faithfulness," she whispered as Ralph rejoined her on the porch.

"What was that?" he asked.

She shivered and stepped back into the kitchen. "Nothing, honey. Just thinking about something you said."

He grinned and turned the lock on the door and put out the light. Some things were easy to keep at bay, like cold breezes and nighttime pests, Anne thought, watching him. And others tended to spring up unwanted and unexpected, and usually at the most inopportune times.

Chapter Twenty-Four

THE BUZZING OF ANNE'S PHONE on her nightstand woke her early the next morning. Time to get up already? She moaned and cracked open one eyelid to glance at the clock. Five thirty! She must have forgotten to turn off her alarm.

"Oomph." She rolled onto her side and jammed her pillow over her head. She didn't want to get up. And besides, it was Saturday. She didn't work on Saturdays.

"Sweetheart? You gonna answer that?" Ralph mumbled. He reached over to give her a shake.

Anne blinked her eyes open and peeked out from under the pillow. "Huh?"

"Your phone. It's ringing."

"I thought it was my alarm." She listened a second. "I don't hear it anymore."

"That's because it's on vibrate."

Actually, it was because by now, the phone had gone silent. "Whoever it was will call back." She sighed and let her eyes drift closed. Only to jerk them open when the phone resumed buzzing.

"Who in the world is calling at this hour—?"

Lili? Had something happened on the way home? Wide awake now, she fumbled for the phone and flipped it over to see the screen.

Not Lili, Shirley—which also was not a good sign since lately, every time she called it was to share more bad news.

Tossing off the covers, Anne hit the answer button then stumbled out of bed. "Hey, Shirley."

"Hey, Anne. Sorry to wake you."

"No, no, it's fine. Is everything okay?" Anne's mind flitted to Shirley's mother, Regina. "What's going on?"

"Seamus called from the hospital last night. It was late, or I would have called you after I talked to him."

Anne stepped into the hall where she could pace without disturbing Ralph. "Seamus, from security?"

"Mm-hmm." A deep sigh sounded on the other end of the line. "He called to let me know there was another mugging."

Anne froze in her tracks. "Oh no. Oh, Shirley."

"I know. I felt exactly the same way when I heard."

Anne ran her free hand over her forehead. When would it stop? "Was anyone hurt?"

"I don't know. Seamus didn't have any details. He just called because he figured I'd want to know."

"Of course. That was nice of him."

"I'm going to head down there in a little bit," Shirley continued. "I was wondering if you'd like to meet me."

"Yeah. Yes, I can do that." Anne glanced down at her rumpled pajamas. "What time?"

"Maybe around seven? That's what time Seamus gets off, and I was hoping to catch him before he leaves for the day."

"Seven. Okay. I'll meet you outside the security office."

"Good. Thanks, Anne."

Anne reached up to scratch her head behind her ear. "What about Evelyn and Joy? Should I call them?"

"Just to let them know what happened? Yeah, that would probably be good. But maybe text them. And I'm not sure about asking them to meet us. I don't want Seamus to feel like we're bombarding him."

"All right. I'll see you in a little bit."

Shirley said goodbye and once they'd hung up, Anne hurried to shower and dress.

Another mugging. Another mugging. Another mugging.

The words added to the pounding in her temples as she pulled into her parking space at the hospital. Who was it this time? A nurse or someone else? Someone who'd been on duty the night Preston brought his son to the hospital? Much as she hated that another person had gone through the same pain and fear as Shirley, Anne couldn't help but wonder if they'd finally get the break they needed to nab the culprit.

Shirley was already outside the security office and talking to Seamus by the time Anne arrived. She hurried forward as Shirley held out her hand to her.

"Here she is."

"Am I late?"

"No, no." Seamus pushed back the sleeve on his uniform and held up his wrist to look at his watch. "You're early. I've still got ten minutes left on my shift."

"I just couldn't stand the wait anymore," Shirley said to Anne. To Seamus, she added, "And I didn't want to risk missing you before you left for the day."

He nodded in understanding. "Come into the office. I'll go over what I know."

The smell of burnt coffee lingered inside the small room. Seamus shrugged out of his yellow reflector vest then held up a stained pot that still had about a quarter left sloshing in the bottom. "Either of you like a cup?"

"No, thanks," Anne said.

Shirley shook her head.

Seamus poured himself a mug and carried it to the desk without adding anything to it, then motioned to a couple of chairs. "So we got the call yesterday evening."

"Same time as the others?" Shirley asked as she sat.

He nodded. "Just after eight."

Anne was too wired to sit. She clutched the top of her chair. "Where did the attack happen this time?"

"Behind the hospital, near the harbor." Seamus crossed one long leg over the other. "Same MO as last time—the attacker came from behind, struck the person, and left."

"So, nothing taken then." Shirley frowned.

Seamus confirmed this, then grimaced and put both feet on the floor, his arms atop the desk. "There was one difference with this attack."

Anne caught her breath as she and Shirley glanced at each other.

"The victim was Nora Burns. Either of you know her?"

"No—" Shirley began.

Anne cut her off. "Nora, from custodial?" Instantly, an image of the sweet little old lady in the gray sweater jumped to her mind.

Seamus raised his brows. "That's her. How do you—?"

"I went down there to talk to Benny's boss," Anne said to Shirley, who nodded. Anne looked at Seamus. "You said something was different about this attack?"

"Afraid so. Ms. Burns had to be admitted for an elevated heart rate after giving her statement to the police." He lifted one hand. "Now, it may have just been her age. She is the oldest victim to date. But she did have some pretty nasty scrapes and bruises on her hands from when she fell, and the doctor thinks she may have messed up her knee when she hit the pavement."

"But her injuries weren't from a blow delivered by the attacker?" Shirley said.

"Not exactly, no. The attacker didn't hit her head like they did you. Ms. Burns said she felt a strong smack across her back and shoulders. That's what drove her to the ground."

Anne drew in a deep breath. "Poor Nora."

"But it does sort of confirm my idea that the attacker wasn't trying to hurt me," Shirley said.

Seamus angled his head to look at her. "I'm sorry?"

Shirley repeated to him what she'd told Anne about her feeling that the attack on her wasn't intended to do any lasting harm. "It wasn't anything the person did, really, other than sticking around for a couple of seconds after I fell. Still, it made me think they were checking on me."

"And the shoes," Anne added. "Tell him about the white shoes the attacker was wearing."

"They could have been nursing shoes," Shirley said. "But I'm not sure that's what they were. Really, all I can remember is that they were white." She looked at Seamus. "I only got a very quick glimpse of them before the person ran off."

White shoes. Not necessarily the kind nurses wore. Anne pondered this while Shirley went on.

What other kind of shoes were white? Tennis shoes? Possibly. Her heart rate quickened. Preston had been wearing tennis shoes the night she went by his house. They were a little battered if she remembered correctly, but they were most definitely white.

Anne jumped as her phone buzzed in her pocket.

Shirley quirked an eyebrow at her. "Everything okay?"

"Yeah." Anne pulled her phone out and saw a number she didn't recognize. "I'm going to step into the hall to take this. Will you be all right for a minute?"

"Of course." Shirley shooed her off.

Anne answered the call as she moved out of the office. "Hello?"

"Anne Mabry, please."

"This is Anne."

"Mrs. Mabry, this is Earl Sheffield. I'm sorry to call so early, but I've had a whole lot of stuff land in my lap this morning."

"I heard. I'm so sorry about Nora."

"Thank you." He sounded a little surprised that news of the attack on his employee had spread so fast, but he recovered quickly. "I appreciate that. Nora is a good employee and great person. I hate that this happened to her."

"Me too," Anne said. "I don't know her well, but I did get a chance to talk to her the other day when I went down to your office. She seemed very nice."

"She is, and a very loyal employee." He cleared his throat. "So Nora said you were asking about Benny Pierce?"

Anne glanced up and down the hall. It was empty, but she lowered her voice anyway. "Yes, that's right. Mr. Pierce said he hurt his hand at work? I was just wondering if you could confirm that for me."

"Uh…" There was rustling in the background, like the sound of paper being shuffled. "I'm sorry, do you work for HR? Is this about his Worker's Comp claim?"

"Oh no. Nothing like that." She waited. Sometimes, it was better to say too little than too much.

"Okay, well…I mean, yeah. He cut it on a broken bottle someone had thrown into the garbage."

"Uh-huh. So was it a scrape, or something else?"

"I wouldn't call it a scrape. He grabbed ahold of the trash bag and didn't realize he'd cut himself until it was too late."

"So he injured his palm then?" Picturing what he described, she said it aloud without actually thinking about it.

"That's right."

"But he's still able to work?"

"Some jobs, yeah. I'm giving him the lighter duty stuff until his hand heals. It was a pretty bad gash. Took about twenty stitches to close him up."

"I see." Anne fell silent, thinking. That many stitches across his palm might have made it difficult and in fact downright painful for him to be involved in this latest attack. She thanked Mr. Sheffield for his time and then disconnected and went back into the security office, where Shirley was still deep in conversation with Seamus. At his elbow, his coffee sat untouched.

"It's the weirdest thing," Seamus said, scratching his head and frowning. "We don't have a single solid lead, even with the extra security. Whoever this attacker is, they've been two steps ahead of us and the police since this started."

The lines of worry creasing Shirley's brow deepened. "Speaking of the police, have they said anything about possible motives?"

Seamus leaned back in the chair and laced his hands over his belly. "Not that I've heard. 'Course, they could be keeping some of their intel close to the vest, just to protect their investigation."

"Yeah, I guess that's right." Shirley sighed and looked at Anne. She pointed to her cell phone. "Who was that who called?"

"Benny's supervisor." Anne wiggled the phone then pushed it back into her purse. "Looks like we're going to have to rule him out as a sus—" She cut short and glanced at Seamus.

"Don't mind me." He laughed and bumped forward in the chair then tapped the desk with his forefinger. "I've heard a lot about the reputation you ladies have. The way I look at it, we can use all the help we can get."

"In that case…" Anne relaxed a little and grinned. "We thought Benny Pierce might possibly be a person of interest in this case. Our suspicions grew when we heard the fifth victim fought off the attacker with her keys. Benny showed up with a cut on his hand, but his supervisor just confirmed that it happened at work. He said it was a pretty significant gash—twenty stitches or something like that—which means it's unlikely he could have been involved in the incident last night."

"Interesting." Seamus leaned back in his chair, the wheels of which were in desperate need of grease. "Mind if I ask who else is on your radar?"

Anne glanced at Shirley, who nodded. Shirley knew Seamus much better than Anne did, so if she thought he could be trusted, that was all Anne needed to know.

"Right now, we're considering a few people. Marilyn Dodson is one."

Seamus's eyes lit with curiosity. "Dr. Seybold's secretary?"

"That's her."

He rubbed his chin in what appeared to be deep thought. "What would be her motive?"

Anne felt a little uncomfortable answering this question since they still weren't sure Marilyn was involved. But if it could be of help in stopping these attacks, she had to share what she knew. She told Seamus about the promotions Marilyn had been passed over for, and how her bitterness had led to her verbally bashing other hospital employees.

"I thought it might be a leap for her to go from talking about people to attacking them," Anne finished, "until I saw her jabbing that letter opener into her desk calendar. Now, I'm not so sure."

Seamus shook his head. "Sorry, Anne, but I'm afraid that road is a dead end."

Shirley looked at him with surprise. "What do you mean?"

He tapped the phone on the end of the desk. "A friend of mine told me Marilyn got a job over at County General. She starts next week." His brow arched. "Looks like Dr. Seybold is gonna be looking for a new secretary, not that he'll mind. He's been pretty vocal about his dissatisfaction with her work."

Anne frowned. "So that's two suspects off our list."

"But speaking of Dr. Seybold…" Shirley's lips thinned, and she raised her eyebrows. "And the ex-Mrs. Seybold, for that matter."

Seamus raised his hand. "No need to say more about either of those two. I've heard plenty of complaints. Trust me, we're already looking into them."

Anne cleared her throat. "Well, then there's Preston Winder."

Seamus rubbed his hand across the back of his neck and sighed. "Sad case, right there. Can't say I blame you for keeping him on your list of suspects. The man has a temper, but he was pretty broken when he lost his son." He lifted one eyebrow and looked at Shirley. "I understand the hospital is still fighting the medical malpractice claims."

"It's not just the claims." Anne went on to tell Seamus about her encounters with Preston. "He had his keys in his hand and was leaving his house when I drove by," she said. "There wasn't an attack that night, but it was just about the right time. We think I may have disrupted his plan."

"Or maybe he couldn't find the right victim," Shirley added.

"Oh, and one more thing." Anne clasped her hands in her lap. "One of the days Preston came by the hospital, he had a folder full of letters and newspaper clippings about the muggings. I know that's circumstantial, but I still found it interesting that he was collecting them."

Seamus nodded thoughtfully.

"We haven't told the police any of this because we didn't feel like we had enough evidence," Shirley said.

"I think that's probably a good call," Seamus said. "I mean, the man's got motive, but as far as evidence, well…" He shrugged and lifted his hands. "Still, I'll pass the information along to one of my buddies on the force. If they are considering Preston, maybe some of this can help."

"Thank you, Seamus," Anne said.

"Of course."

"And thanks for letting us know about this latest mugging." Shirley rose and shook Seamus's hand.

"No problem. You take care, Shirley. You too, Anne."

Anne and Shirley made their way to the cafeteria for some coffee. It wasn't busy, and they quickly found a table.

"So?" Shirley asked as they pulled out their chairs and sat. "What do you think?"

"At this point, who knows?" Anne tore the top off a packet of low-calorie sweetener and swirled it into her coffee. "I'm so frustrated, Shirley. Every time I think we're making headway, something springs up to derail us."

Shirley peeled back the tab on the lid of her coffee cup and took a careful sip. "I admit, this one has me stumped. Can't tell the wheat from the tares."

Anne tasted her coffee, grimaced, and added a second sweetener. "On another subject, have you thought about when you're coming back to work?"

"I have. I think the doctor will release me to return next week if I want to. Of course, I think the hospital will want me to go to counseling for PTSD before I do."

Anne raised her eyebrows. "Will you?"

"Go to counseling?"

Anne shook her head. "Come back to work."

"I love my job too much not to. Mama's worried, of course, but I told her I'd be careful not to walk out alone."

"That's probably wise even if this hadn't happened."

Shirley nodded her agreement as she fingered the rim of her Styrofoam cup. "You know what bothers me most about this whole thing? The fact that the hospital doesn't feel as safe as it used to. I'm checking over my shoulder more, listening for footsteps behind me. I feel like something's been stolen from me and I'm not sure how long it's going to take to get it back."

"That will fade with time," Anne said.

"I sure hope so."

Shirley's gaze drifted slowly over the cafeteria. Anne's followed. She took it all in—the doctors and nurses hurrying back and forth with their trays, the clatter of dishes being stacked in dispensers, the smell of bacon and eggs mixed with donuts and coffee.

"I love this place," Shirley continued. "I don't want what happened to change how I feel. But I'm worried. I think it'll be a while before things can return to normal."

And part of that would be tracking down the person behind the attacks and stopping them for good. "We'll figure out what's going on, Shirl," Anne promised. "Joy, Evelyn, and I—we won't stop until we do."

Shirley covered Anne's hand with her own. "I know you won't. I'm grateful for each and every one of you."

"And we're grateful for you."

Shirley smiled and looked at her watch. "I should be going. I know I've said it before, but Mama will be wondering where I am.

I feel like I'm a teenager again. Lately, I can't even leave the room without making her nervous."

Poor Regina. And Shirley. This attack had taken a toll on them both.

"All right, but before you go..." Anne stood up and wrapped Shirley in a firm hug. Though she knew it was lasting too long, she couldn't seem to let go. Didn't want to. Finally, she dropped her arms and took a step back. "Be careful, okay? I'll talk to you tonight."

"Okay. Bye, Anne."

"Bye." Anne forced a smile as she watched Shirley weave her way out of the cafeteria, waving when she stopped by the entrance to look back at her. Only when she ducked out of sight did Anne let the smile slip from her lips and her real emotions show.

She blew out a long, shuddering breath. She was mad. Madder than she'd been in a long time. At the situation. At the attacker for targeting her friend. And at herself for not solving this case. But that was going to change because she wouldn't stop. Not until she had answers. For herself. And for Shirley.

Chapter Twenty-Five

ONE WEEK. ANNE FINGERED THE top of her leather Bible cover and stared out the car window. It was hard to believe a full week had passed since she'd determined not to give up until she had answers and she still felt no closer to figuring out who the hospital attacker was or how to stop them. As she and Ralph drove to church, Anne couldn't help but wonder what she was doing wrong and why God seemed so strangely silent on the topic.

Seeing the sunlight sparkling on Charleston Harbor, the blue sky overhead making the water shine like glass, she found it odd to think of God as silent…or distant. How could a Creator responsible for all of this beauty be either of those things? But that was how she felt and there was no getting around it.

Ralph let go of the steering wheel with one hand and rested it on her knee. "You okay, hon? You're awfully quiet this morning."

"I'm fine." She turned from the window to look at her husband then shook her head. That wasn't true. "Just preoccupied, I guess."

"Anything I can do to help?"

Dear Ralph. She hadn't meant to worry him with her melancholy. She reached out to smooth the earnest lines from his face. "No, but thanks for offering."

He nodded, and they drove the rest of the way in silence.

Inside the church, seeing the smiling faces of so many dear friends, she felt her mood lift. A little. She put on an answering smile for the people she greeted, lifted her hand for the prayer requests, and nodded her agreement during the sermon. She was present, engaged even, and yet...it all felt strangely hollow.

"These people honor me with their lips, but their hearts are far from me."

Anne blinked and looked at Ralph. "What?"

From the pew in front of them, a woman cast a frown of disapproval over her shoulder. Ralph whispered an apology then eyed Anne with a mixture of curiosity and surprise.

She'd spoken too loudly. Anne leaned toward him and lowered her voice. "Did you say something?"

"No." He angled his head to look into her face. "Are you okay?"

She nodded and settled back against her seat. She'd been so sure she'd heard him speak.

"'They worship me in vain; their teachings are merely human rules.'"

Anne directed her gaze to the pulpit, where the pastor read from his Bible. She relaxed a little. So that was what she heard. Not Ralph. The pastor.

"Is our worship in vain this morning?" the pastor continued, peering at the congregation over the top of a pair of black-framed glasses. "Are we praising God with our lips, but in our hearts"—he paused and touched his chest—"are we holding something back? Something precious? Something we can't quite let go of because we don't really trust Him?"

Anne sucked in a breath and looked at the people around her. Most listened with looks of interest on their faces. A couple scrolled through their phones. One girl doodled on the church bulletin. Somehow, Anne felt the message wasn't for them.

She riffled through the pages in her Bible until she found the passage the pastor had read.

"These people honor me with their lips, but their hearts are far from me. They worship me in vain; their teachings are merely human rules."

Their *hearts* were far from God.

Anne grabbed a yellow highlighter out of her purse, then marked the word and circled it. The truth of that one line speared her to the marrow. Was she holding something back? She didn't think so. She'd given her heart to God a long time ago. She loved and served him. She trusted Him.

Didn't she?

Her mouth went dry. She'd always thought so, but lately she'd been fighting feelings of anger and disappointment. And why?

The answer came thundering out like water from a floodgate.

It was because sometimes the answer God gave wasn't the answer she wanted. And because she couldn't always see His plan, which meant she had to trust Him blindly. That was all right for herself, but it was much harder with the people she loved. The ones she held tightly to for fear of losing.

There it was—the whole ugly truth she'd kept buried deep inside. The moment she acknowledged it, put words to the feelings that had been roiling around inside her, she felt better. Lighter. Like she'd cleaned out a festering wound and could finally begin to heal.

"I'm sorry, Lord." It was the barest little whisper, but it came straight from her heart. "I'm sorry I keep taking back what I promised to give to You."

And what she'd promised was everything. For several minutes, Anne sat in silent prayer, pouring out what she'd tried in vain to keep pent up. When she'd finally finished, when she felt spent and emptied, she opened her eyes and saw her husband beside her, his head bent. Still praying. Still holding her hand—she hadn't even realized when he'd taken it—and crying. Because she'd been crying. Weeping with her. Over her. Even though he didn't know what was wrong. Or maybe he did know even before she did.

The last worship song ended. Ralph opened his eyes and looked straight at her. "Okay?"

She nodded and he drew her close, against his chest, next to his heart. She couldn't have asked for a more perfect picture of what had just happened between her and Jesus. It was all going to be okay. She could rest now, not because the circumstances had changed, but because she had, or was still. She didn't have all the answers, but God did. He was faithful. He'd proven that time and again over the years. And she trusted Him.

She smiled against her husband's shirt. She'd probably need to remind herself of this several times over the next few days, but that was okay, because her Father was patient. And He loved her. If she ever doubted the truth of that statement, she had only to look into her husband's eyes.

For today, it was enough.

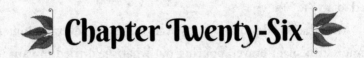

Chapter Twenty-Six

"I WILL NOT TAKE BACK what I've given to You, Lord."

Anne repeated the statement to herself several times over the course of the following Monday. Having admitted to herself the fear she'd been harboring in her heart, Anne had no desire to take it back up.

So when Lili called and said Addie still wasn't well enough to return to school, Anne prayed and trusted God with her care. And when she found Aurora crying in the locker room because David had called and said he wouldn't be coming back from Detroit, Anne prayed with her and told her what she'd learned about trusting God. And when Shirley arrived at the hospital for their workout and Anne still didn't have an answer as to who had attacked her, she wasn't angry or disappointed because this too was part of God's plan.

Walking into the fitness studio with a gym bag slung over her shoulder, Shirley eyed her curiously. "You're different today. Something happen at work?"

Anne smiled. "Actually, it happened at church. Remind me to tell you about it after class."

"Mm-hmm." Shirley's wink said she already had a pretty good idea of what Anne was going to say, at least the part that involved God. She motioned toward the door as Evelyn and Joy walked in.

"There are the girls. Did you have a chance to tell them about our talk with Seamus?"

Anne winced and ducked her head. "I'm ashamed to say I didn't. I'm sorry, Shirl. I meant to call over the weekend, but I just forgot. And today has been—"

Shirley cut her off with a wave. "No worries. I've been distracted too. Let's go fill them in."

Anne followed as Shirley led the way. Together, they told them about what Seamus had said about Marilyn's new job, and what Anne had learned about Benny's hand.

Evelyn rubbed her fingers over her brow. "That's two suspects off our list. Who does that leave?"

"I think the obvious choice has to be Preston," Joy said, bracing both hands on her hips. "We've said all along he has the most motive."

Pressing her lips together, Anne looked away. "Yeah, but something about that situation seems off to me."

Fidgeting with the zipper on her jacket, Evelyn cleared her throat. "You don't think that might be because of your similar history?"

She was trying to be delicate, and Anne appreciated her for it. "I thought so, at first. Now I'm just not sure Preston had the opportunity. I mean, what about the cameras?"

"That's right." Shirley rubbed her chin as though deep in thought. "Preston's been to the hospital a lot lately, but enough to figure out where all the security cameras are and avoid them? I mean, I work here, and I'm not sure I could say where all the cameras are located. Figuring that out would require some planning."

"Which maybe doesn't fit with the scenario that he's just gotten tired of waiting for the system to run its course?" Joy added, hesitation in her voice. She looked from Shirley, to Evelyn, and finally to Anne.

"So, if it's not Preston—" Anne began.

"Um, sorry." All four heads turned to Talia. She bent forward a little as she looked at them, lifted her gloved hand, and wiggled her fingers. "Class is about to start. We're going to be working with weights today, so if you prefer to use gloves, now is the time to put them on."

"Oh." Shirley looked down at her hands. "I didn't bring any—"

"No worries." Talia smiled and waved toward the back. "I've got extras if you want them. They're in the box on my desk. Help yourself."

"Okay. Thanks."

"I'm going to get some too," Evelyn said.

"And me." Joy shrugged in apology. "I never thought to buy gloves."

"It's no problem." Talia laughed and jerked her thumb over her shoulder. "I have plenty."

All four ladies moved in the direction she pointed. As Anne passed, Talia touched her elbow.

"Hey, uh, have you got a second?"

Again? Anticipating that she was going to ask if she'd talked to Dr. Seybold, Anne felt a pang of guilt. She stopped and turned to Talia.

"I couldn't help overhearing y'all," Talia said. "You were talking about the attacks that have happened here at the hospital, weren't you?"

The question caught Anne by surprise. "Um, yeah, as a matter of fact, we were."

Talia shifted her weight to one foot, worry adding lines to her otherwise flawless skin. "I heard there was another one Friday night."

Anne wasn't surprised that she'd heard. It was the talk of the hospital, taking precedence over everything else. "Yeah, there was. It happened behind the hospital, near the harbor."

"That's too bad." Talia bit her lip. "Have they said, I mean, do they have any idea who did it?"

"I'm afraid not," Anne said.

Talia puffed out a breath, and her shoulders fell. "Sorry. I guess I'm a little disappointed. I heard you talking about some guy named Preston and I thought…well…anyway." She stopped and flicked her dark hair over her shoulder.

Anne eyed her curiously. Some guy? Hadn't she overheard Julie talking to Talia about Preston? It wasn't a common name. Surely she remembered him?

Talia licked her lips. "So, on another subject…have you had a chance to talk to Marcus?"

"Dr. Seybold? Afraid not. I went by his office, but he was on his way to surgery and there wasn't time."

To Anne's surprise, Talia looked relieved. "That's all right. I'm glad it didn't work out." She shrugged. "He hasn't been by since that last time, so maybe he finally got the hint." Her voice lifted at the end, as though she wasn't quite sure but was trying very hard to convince herself it was true.

"I hope so." Anne flashed an awkward smile. This wasn't something she was comfortable talking about.

"I guess there's a first time for everything, right?" Talia sneered. "Some people think they're better than everyone else."

The change in her tone was shocking in that it happened so fast. "And Dr. Seybold is one of those?" Anne asked carefully.

"Ha!" She barked a laugh lacking in humor. "Is he ever. Did you know he dated some of the victims?"

Anne bit her lip and stayed quiet.

Talia bobbed her head in disgust. "The worst thing is the hospital knows about his philandering, but do you think they'll do anything about it?"

Anne glanced toward the door, where a few people had begun trickling in. "Um, well, I have heard he likes to flirt."

"You know, if that was all there is to it, maybe it wouldn't be so bad." She leaned toward Anne and lowered her voice. "But between you and me, I think he's the one police should be paying attention to."

Anne frowned. "Are you saying you think he's…" She trailed off and Talia nodded.

"That's why I've been making sure I'm out of here before he takes his run. I don't have any proof, but I've learned to listen to my gut." She laid her gloved hand over Anne's arm, her large, dark eyes wide and somber. "Right now, it's telling me he's dangerous, so stay away from him if you can." At Anne's nod, she moved back and gestured toward the people gathering by the door. "I should get going."

"Yeah, okay. Thanks for the information, Talia."

"You're welcome." She walked off, a perky bounce to her step as she greeted the other class participants.

Shirley approached, a curious frown on her face as she watched Talia. She glanced at Anne. "What was that all about?"

"I'm not sure exactly."

Evelyn and Joy joined them, and Anne gave them the summarized version of her conversation with Talia.

Evelyn held a pair of gloves out to Anne. "Well, we wondered who else besides Preston should be on our suspect list. Maybe she just gave us the answer."

"Maybe." Anne took the fingerless gloves and wriggled them on. "But we'll think about that after class. For now, I just need to work up some endorphins." She planted her fists on her hips and grinned. "Who's with me?"

Joy jerked her hand into the air and wiggled her fingers. "I'm in, but I'm sticking with the three-pound weights." She laughed and looked at her gloves. "Which I guess kinda makes these things excessive."

Shirley shrugged looked at her gloves, front and back. "Eh. I like them. Makes me feel like I'm about to accomplish something."

She balled one hand into a fist and pounded it into her opposite palm, the resulting smack loud against the leather glove. Evelyn and Joy laughed, and Anne quickly joined in. It felt good, like she'd been letting worry rob her of joy for too long. Grabbing hold of that thought, she threw herself into the class, pushing until she was tired and covered in sweat, but as Shirley had said, like she'd accomplished something.

After the workout, Anne lingered while Joy and Evelyn refilled their water bottles. Shirley also stayed, and Anne looked forward to telling her about what had happened at church.

Anne held out her hands to the other three. "Here, give me your gloves. I saw a laundry bin next to the bathrooms. I'll go turn them in and then we can grab a protein shake or something."

"Sounds good." Evelyn passed her the gloves then used a corner of her towel to wipe the moisture from her forehead.

"It does sound good, but I'm going to have to pass," Joy said. "Sabrina is supposed to call so we can start making plans for Thanksgiving."

"Hard to believe that it's just around the corner," Shirley said, taking her gloves and Joy's and giving them to Anne. "Every year I say I'm going to plan better, and every year it sneaks up on me."

Clutching all of the gloves, Anne laughed and headed toward the bathrooms. The laundry bin was tucked into a corner near the door, just as she'd remembered. She threw the gloves inside, tsking when one missed and landed on the floor behind the bin.

"Aargh." Anne bent over the bin, but even stretching on her tip-toes, the glove was out of reach. Seeing people lining up to toss their towels into the bin, she smiled and stepped aside. "Sorry. Go ahead."

Once the crowd thinned, Anne grabbed the bin and pulled it away from the wall far enough so she could see behind it. Her glove lay in the farthest corner. No wonder she couldn't reach it. Anne yanked the bin out a little farther until she'd made a space large enough to fit her whole arm through. Finally, her fingers closed on the glove. And something else. Something soft.

She pulled it out. A workout shirt? It was dark gray and covered in dust. Obviously the area behind the bin wasn't a space that got swept often. No telling how long the shirt had been there. Anne tossed it and the glove on top of the laundry pile, then shoved the bin back into place. It was then that she noticed something she hadn't before.

The shirt was torn on one sleeve. And that wasn't all. She leaned closer for a better look then jerked back with a gasp. Along the wrist, and dotting the front, was something that looked suspiciously like blood.

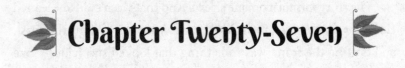

Chapter Twenty-Seven

"Are we sure it's blood?"

Joy, Evelyn, and Shirley huddled around the kitchen table with Anne, all of them peering at the same few specks on the gray shirt Anne had found behind the laundry bin.

"I mean, they're kind of brown," Joy continued. "Maybe it's rust."

Evelyn arched a brow. "And how would rust get on this shirt?"

"And why is it torn?" Shirley added. No one answered.

"It was dusty," Anne said. "I thought it was because it had been back there a long time, but it may have just been from me dragging it through the dust on the floor."

Shirley sat back in her chair. "So? What do we do now? Should we ask Talia about the shirt?"

Anne looked at Evelyn and then Joy, both of whom shrugged. Anne frowned. "We don't *know* this is the shirt the attacker was wearing when Susan was mugged."

Joy lifted one shoulder in a shrug. "For that matter, we don't know it belongs to Talia. Or how the blood got on it, if it really is blood."

"Then I guess the answer is yes, we ask her about it," Anne said, and then gasped and laid both hands on the table, palms down. "The gloves."

Startled, Evelyn pressed her hand to her heart. "What?"

"The CrossFit gloves. I just thought of it." She looked at Joy. "Do you have the workout schedule on your phone?"

"Yeah." Joy slid her cell out of her pocket.

"Check it. See if Talia had weight training listed for today."

"You're thinking she could have been wearing the gloves to hide the scratch from Susan's keys?" Shirley asked.

Anne nodded.

"Um…" Joy swiped up several times and then shook her head. "Nope. Sorry, girls. Here it is on the schedule app, plain as day." She bit her lip and scowled. "Sure feels like I would have remembered though."

"Regardless, hasn't she worn them before?" Evelyn asked.

All three fell silent while they pondered the answer.

"I'm not sure," Joy said finally.

"Me neither," Shirley said. "I never really paid attention."

"All right, so maybe the gloves are a dead end, but we still have the shirt." Anne grimaced. "Or do we? If it is blood, or even if we think it is, we should probably turn it over to the police."

"Before we talk to Talia?" Shirley asked.

Both Evelyn and Joy nodded.

"We do have to consider that they will likely say it's circumstantial," Evelyn said. "Even if it turns out to be blood, people cut themselves on all sorts of things. A locker door. A cracked weight. It is a hospital, after all. This could be entirely coincidental."

"It might still be withholding evidence if the shirt really does belong to the attacker," Joy said, touching Evelyn's hand.

Anne studied their faces. "All right, so we're agreed? We take the shirt to the police and then we talk to Talia?"

All three heads bobbed.

"Good." Anne pushed the shirt aside. "Now, let's talk about motive. If Talia is behind the attacks, what reason could she have?"

"Talia said Dr. Seybold dated some of the victims," Evelyn said, "which I suppose could tie to some sort of motive."

"You mean like jealousy?"

"Possibly. Talia dated him. Maybe she wanted to get these other women out of the way."

"But what about Nora? Why attack her?" Joy asked. "Or Shirley?"

Except for the clicking of Evelyn's nails against the tabletop, no one made a sound.

"Maybe her motive will be clearer after we meet with her," Joy suggested, a hopeful note to her tone that Anne found encouraging.

"Maybe. I guess there's no point worrying about it until then." Anne got up, crossed to a drawer where she kept rolls of aluminum foil and plastic wrap, and dug around until she found a zippered storage bag. She tugged it free, then rummaged through another drawer for a set of tongs and carried both back to the table. Carefully, she lifted the shirt with the tongs and shoved it into the storage bag.

Still holding the tongs, she looked up at the girls. "I guess this is kind of silly seeing as how my hands have been all over it."

"That doesn't mean you shouldn't be conscious of how you handle it now," Joy said, eyeing the shirt as though it might scamper off on its own at any moment.

"Hey, sweetheart—"

All four women jumped as the kitchen door burst open and Ralph stepped inside.

"Ralph, you scared us," Anne scolded.

Ralph lifted both hands in appeasement. "Oh, sorry, I didn't know we had company."

Anne took a deep breath to calm the racing of her heart. "Are you just getting home from the hospital?"

"Uh-huh. Long day. I had several counseling sessions run late." He angled his head at the storage bag and shirt inside. "Hey, what is this?" He reached for it.

"Don't touch it!"

All four women threw up their hands, freezing Ralph in his tracks. He backed away, palms out. "Okay, you know what? I'm just gonna leave you ladies to whatever you were doing." He shot a glance at Anne. "Takeout for supper?"

"I think that would be a good idea," she said, laughing now that she no longer thought Ralph would contaminate the shirt further. When he was gone, she picked up the storage bag by one corner. "I'm going to take this down to the police station before anything happens to it. Anybody want to join me?"

"I'll go," Evelyn said.

Joy nodded. "Me too."

But Shirley was already shaking her head. "You three go on. I'm gonna head home and see to Mama. I hate to be a spoilsport, but it's almost her bedtime, and I don't want to mess up her routine now that she's finally sleeping again."

"She is? Oh, that's good news." Anne set the bag down and walked with Shirley to the door. "I'll call you and let you know what the police have to say."

"Thanks." A frown deepened on Shirley's face. "Listen, Anne—about Talia. When you talk to her, maybe you shouldn't be alone. It could be dangerous. If she's guilty, I mean."

Anne squeezed her arm. "I know. I'll be careful, and I'll be sure to wait until I can take one of y'all with me."

"All right." Shirley patted her hand and then stepped away to get her coat and purse. A moment later, she slipped out the door.

Anne fetched her own coat before rejoining Evelyn and Joy in the kitchen. It was early yet, only a few minutes after eight, but Anne knew Ralph wouldn't like the idea of them heading to the police station alone. She ducked into the living room to let him know what was going on. As expected, he insisted on going with them to the station. They made the drive and were soon sitting inside an inter-rogation room with Jimbo Carson, one of the officers with the Charleston Police Department.

Officer Carson listened patiently while Anne explained what she'd found and where. When she pulled out the storage bag with the shirt inside, he took it and studied the contents.

Finally, he set the bag down and leaned forward over a long wooden table. "While this is interesting, you do understand that it may not be enough to bring Talia Reynolds in for questioning?"

"We were afraid of that," Anne said, "which is why we thought we should also tell you about the gloves."

Officer Carson's jaw clenched as he listened, and his eyes wid-ened slightly, sure clues that he found the information worthy of his attention. Ralph clasped Anne's hand when she finished and shot her an encouraging glance. Anne squeezed his fingers back. What she'd shared might not lead to anything, but she felt good for having done her part to at least try to help.

Officer Carson's vintage steel desk chair squeaked and rattled as he stood. "All right, if you folks will give me just a minute? I need to speak to the chief."

All four of them nodded as he let himself out of the interrogation room, closing the frosted glass door behind him.

When he was gone, Anne blew out a breath. "Well? What did you think?"

"He seemed to be interested," Evelyn said.

"That's what I thought," Joy said. "Especially when you mentioned the gloves. I'm glad you told him that we weren't sure when she started wearing them though. I wouldn't want to create suspicion where there shouldn't be any, but it's certainly worth checking into."

Anne looked at Ralph.

"You did good, hon." He smiled and gave her fingers another squeeze. "Now it's up to the police to decide what they do with the information."

Minutes ticked by on the black-and-white clock mounted over the table where they sat. Several times, footsteps sounded near the door. Each time, they turned their heads. Anne kept expecting Officer Carson and was disappointed when the person passed by. Finally, the door opened and Officer Carson stepped through, a notebook and pen in his hand.

"Sorry about the wait, folks."

Anne nodded eagerly and noticed the others did too.

Officer Carson laid the notebook in front of Anne and held out the pen. "Mrs. Mabry, would you mind leaving your number and a good time to reach you in case I have any questions?"

"Of course not." She took the pen and wrote down her cell phone number, then added Ralph's number below it. When she finished, she extended the pen back to him, but he shook his head and motioned toward Evelyn and Joy.

"Ladies, it might be a good idea if I had your numbers as well, just in case."

They each added their name and phone number to the sheet, and then Anne pushed everything back toward Officer Carson. "Is that it?"

"For now." He tore out the slip of paper, folded it in half, and stuck it in his pocket. "Thank you all so much for coming in."

He looked expectantly toward the door. Anne wanted to ask what the police had planned but figured he wouldn't tell her, and she couldn't blame him. This was an ongoing investigation, much as she wanted to see it over. She stood, her chair scraping against the worn tile floor. Evelyn, Joy, and Ralph all did the same.

"Oh, and Mrs. Mabry, there is one more thing." Officer Carson nodded toward the shirt, still inside the storage bag. "We appreciate your help on this, but it might be best just to let us handle things from here on out, if you know what I mean."

She did. Anne glanced at Evelyn and Joy. So much for talking with Talia. She looked back at Officer Carson and nodded. "I understand. Thank you, Officer."

After she'd retrieved her jacket, she joined the others as they made their way out to the parking lot, with not a word said between them until they stood near their cars. Rather than going all the way back to Anne and Ralph's, they'd opted to drive separately.

"Well, that was disappointing." Evelyn tugged her keys from her purse and hit the unlock button on her car. It chirped, and then the soft yellow glow from her headlights cut narrow circles on the dark pavement.

"I don't know what I expected," Anne said, leaning against the side of Evelyn's car. "I guess I figured they'd go straight to Talia for questioning." Her phone buzzed in her pocket. She had switched it to vibrate when they entered the police station and had forgotten to turn the ringer back on.

"They still might," Joy said. "Officer Carson did say to leave the rest to them, which sounds like maybe they're planning on doing something."

Ralph nudged Anne's arm. "Your phone is ringing."

"It's probably Shirley. I told her we would call once we were done." Anne dug in her pocket for her phone and pulled it out. Sure enough, the caller ID flashed Shirley's name. Anne showed them and then swiped to answer.

"Hey, Shirley. We just left the police station."

"Yeah? Well, you may want to hang around a little longer."

Tension thrummed in Shirley's voice, putting Anne on her guard. She clutched the phone tighter. "Why? What happened?"

At those words, Evelyn, Joy, and Ralph instantly snapped to attention. They circled close, all of them staring at Anne with wide eyes.

Anne jerked the phone away from her ear and hit the speaker button. "Shirley? I have you on speaker now. Can you repeat what you just said?"

"I said it's Talia." A quaver shook Shirley's voice, making it weak. "Someone just attacked her outside of the hospital."

Chapter Twenty-Eight

FOR SEVERAL SECONDS, NO ONE spoke. Anne finally managed a whisper. "What did you just say?"

In fact, she'd heard what Shirley said, she just needed someone to repeat it.

"Talia was attacked," Joy said, filling in when Shirley didn't speak.

Anne cleared her throat. She wanted to know details, but she asked the most important one. "Is she okay? Was she hurt?"

"She's okay. She's still in the emergency room getting checked out, but Garrison said he didn't think she had any serious injuries, just some scrapes and bruises."

Ralph pressed closer to Anne's side and leaned forward to speak into the phone. "Will they keep her overnight?"

"I'm not sure. I guess that'll depend on where her injuries are and whether or not Talia has someone to look after her. If it's a head wound, like mine, they'll more than likely want to keep her so they can monitor for a concussion."

The knots in Anne's stomach tightened. "We should probably go back inside and let Officer Carson know what's happened."

"I'll do it." Ralph squeezed her shoulder and then turned and hurried toward the station, his shadow long and narrow in the beam cast by Evelyn's headlights.

Anne looked at Evelyn and Joy and shuddered. "I feel terrible. We just told Officer Carson that we thought Talia was the attacker."

"We made a mistake," Joy said, her voice gentle. "I'm sure he'll understand."

"I'm just glad we didn't talk to Talia," Evelyn said.

"We should go see her," Anne said, then turned the phone to her mouth. "Shirley, did Garrison say anything more about what happened?"

"Afraid not. He was headed back to the hospital when he called."

Anne glanced at her watch. "Okay, well, it's getting late. Did he say if he would call you once he's had a chance to learn more?"

"No, but I don't think he will. I assume he'll just wait until morning." Shirley's voice dropped to a whisper. "I think I hear Mama stirring. I should check on her."

"Okay, we'll let you go. In the meantime, we'll just plan on visiting Talia tomorrow." Anne looked at Evelyn and Joy for confirmation, and both of them nodded. "Talk to you later, Shirley."

"Bye, girls." She disconnected.

Anne stared at the dark screen a second longer then straightened with a sigh. "How's that old saying go? Back to square one?"

Evelyn snorted in the exact same instant that the timer on the car turned the headlights off. She clicked the button on her key fob to turn them on again, then looked at Anne. "At this point, square one would feel like we're getting somewhere. This feels like we're not even on the playing board."

It was a pretty dim perspective, but it was exactly how Anne felt. They waited until Ralph returned and then went their separate ways, Anne pondering what they'd do when morning came. For her, that was around four thirty. Unable to sleep for the images circling inside her head, she got up, brushed her teeth, then went down to the kitchen to start a pot of coffee. Ralph joined her just a few minutes later and circled around behind her to rub her shoulders.

"Couldn't sleep, huh?"

"No." Anne sighed and rubbed her fingers wearily over her eyelids. "Did I wake you with my tossing and turning?"

He pressed a kiss to her neck, then reached into the cupboard for two mugs. "I was already awake. I just kept thinking about what you told me about Talia."

While the coffee brewed, Ralph took Anne's hand and pulled her to the table. "Let's sit down and talk about it some more. Maybe we'll stumble onto something we didn't before."

Anne tried to smile but decided it wasn't worth the effort. "I don't know, Ralph. I've gone over every detail in my head at least a thousand times."

He kissed her fingers and made exaggerated puppy-dog eyes at her. "Make it one thousand and one?"

This time, she did laugh. And roll her eyes. "Fine."

They sat down, but Ralph immediately jumped up. "Hold on." He scrounged in one of the drawers until he found a notepad and pen, and then he brought them to the table. "All right, I'm ready."

Anne shook her head. "How you have this much energy in the morning, I'll never know."

He wiggled his eyebrows. "So, start with suspects?"

She ticked them off on her fingers. "Preston, Dr. Seybold, and his wife. That's all we have left."

Ralph wrote the three names on the paper. "Motives?"

He was really getting into this. She angled her head at him and tapped the paper. "You know Preston's."

He nodded and wrote "son" next to Preston's name. "Dr. Seybold?"

"Petty jealousy?" Anne lifted her hands helplessly.

Ralph wrote the word next to Dr. Seybold's name then took her hand and peered at her steadily. "Come on now. Let's think this through. What makes you believe he's the jealous type?"

Anne rubbed her chin. "Maybe *jealous* isn't the right word."

"Grudging? Bitter? Desirous?"

After each word, Anne shook her head.

"Salacious, greedy—"

"Salacious." She grabbed his arm to stop him. "Isn't that what the Bible calls lascivious?"

Ralph nodded. "They're close cousins. Why?"

She lowered her hand, thinking. "I think that's what people mean when they talk about Dr. Seybold's reputation. But there's something else. An element of competitiveness that makes him keep going after something until he gets what he wants."

The coffee maker hissed and gurgled, indicating that the coffee had finished brewing. Ralph rose and poured some into each of the mugs and carried them back to the table. "Well, he is a surgeon. I suppose there would have to be something about his character that would make him motivated to push himself."

Anne shoved the paper toward him. "Write that down. *Motivated*. No, put *driven*."

Ralph slid the cream and sugar toward Anne then jotted both words while she swirled the condiments into their cups. Afterward, he took a sip and sighed happily. "Mmm. That's good." He clicked the end of the pen with his thumb. "Okay, so I guess we've covered all of Dr. Seybold's faults. How exactly does any of that tie to his possible motive?"

"Well, we could say all of the victims either denied him something or stood in his way," Anne said.

Ralph's brows rose. "Including Talia?"

A flutter of excitement started in her stomach as she leaned into the idea that Dr. Seybold might be guilty. She held up one finger.

"Actually, yes. I saw him coming out of the fitness studio one day. He said he was there checking things out, but when I asked him if he was joining the class, he said he preferred running"—she slapped her hand against the table—"which he does every evening at eight o'clock." Her voice rose. "And after he left the studio, Talia came out with her makeup all smudged. I thought it was because she'd been crying, but Evelyn suggested maybe it was just because she'd been sweating from the last workout, so I let it drop. Now I'm thinking my first instinct was right."

She froze as a new thought struck. "Her necklace." She fluttered her fingers to her throat. "Talia's necklace. She told me she'd gotten it in the Bahamas. Later, I saw a picture of Dr. Seybold taken in the same place. What if they went there together?"

"Okay, but I'm not sure I'm following—"

"Talia said they broke up but that Dr. Seybold has been trying to win her back." Anne sat forward in excitement. "Talia didn't want that, which makes me think maybe she's the one who broke it off. She even asked me to talk to him because she was afraid she'd lose her job if she went to HR. Maybe Dr. Seybold didn't want to take no for an answer. Maybe he was 'driven'"—she used air quotes to emphasize her point—"to go after her when she refused to give in to his advances, but he had to cover his tracks so he targeted a few random victims first."

"And last night was the culmination of that?"

"One way to find out." She pushed up from the table, but Ralph grabbed her hand to keep her from leaving.

"Sweetheart."

"What? Ralph, I need to talk to Talia."

He gave a toss of his chin toward the clock. "It's five in the morning."

She crossed her arms, chagrined. "No it's not. It's almost five thirty."

"Still too early to be running to the hospital." He nudged her coffee toward her. "Might as well drink up."

Much as she hated to admit it, he was right. She sank back into her chair. "Fine. One cup," she said and smiled as she clasped her husband's fingers. "And thank you."

Eyes twinkling, he peered at her over the rim of his mug. "For what?"

You know what popped into her brain, but she didn't say it. Instead, she reached for her mug and saluted him with it. "For this. I just love a good cup of coffee."

He chuckled, and they talked a little more until the sky blushed with color. Then Anne hurried upstairs to wash and change before heading to the hospital. When she arrived, visiting hours had not quite started, but everyone at the hospital knew Anne, so she quickly got a room number for Talia. Swinging toward the elevators, she said a quick prayer for peace and wisdom before climbing on board and riding the car up.

Lights in the hall outside Talia's door were bright, but through a slight crack, Anne could see the inside of the room was dim, with only one lamp spilling light across the floor. She hesitated to knock. If Talia was sleeping, she didn't want to disturb her, especially after such a traumatic night.

"Is someone there?"

Anne paused with her hand on the brushed silver handle. "Talia?"

"Oh, Anne. Come on in."

Anne pushed the door open just as Talia shifted upright in the bed, the covers sliding to her waist. The room was bare. No flowers on the nightstand. No *Get Well Soon* cards on the windowsill. It could be because she'd only been admitted a few hours ago, Anne reasoned, but she still instantly regretted not stopping by the gift shop before she came up.

"Come on in," Talia repeated, gesturing for her to come closer. Her eyes were red and sunken, her skin pale against the white sheets. "Thank you so much for coming to see me."

"Of course."

Anne shrugged out of her coat and draped it over her arm as she approached the bed. Talia's hair was in a ponytail, and her head was wrapped in a gauze bandage. The soft fluorescent light over her bed also revealed a scrape on one cheek and bandages over both palms.

"How are you?" Anne asked. The entire floor was so quiet, she felt compelled to whisper.

Talia sniffled and slowly extended her hand toward the box of tissues on her bedside table. Anne hurried to get them for her. "Here you go."

"Thank you." Talia took one and pressed it to her nose. "Last night was tough, but I'm doing better this morning."

Anne tried not to stare at the dark circles under Talia's eyes. This was better? She smiled in sympathy. "Were you able to get any sleep?"

"Not really." Her eyes filled with tears, which she dabbed with the tissue. "I jumped at every little noise, which is why I heard you outside the door."

"Sure." Anne nodded. "I'm so sorry this happened, Talia. Is there anyone I can call for you? Anything you need me to do? I can post a sign outside the studio, if you need me to, letting people know that classes will be postponed for a while."

"Thanks, but there's no need." She pointed to a phone hooked to a charger plugged into the wall. "I use the app. I've already sent out an update."

"Oh. I didn't realize it was so easy."

Talia nodded and wiped the tissue under her nose, then she dropped it onto the tray table and tugged another from the box.

Anne cleared her throat. "So, if you're feeling up to it, would you mind if I asked you a few questions?"

Talia lowered the tissue warily. "Questions?"

"About what happened last night."

"Um…" She put her hand to her mouth and glanced toward the door. "I've already told the police everything I can remember."

Anne grabbed a nearby chair and dragged it closer. "I know, but there's something I'd like your input on. I think it might be important to solving this case."

Talia still appeared hesitant, but she nodded, so Anne sat down and folded her hands in her lap. "Let's start with last night. Can you tell me what happened?"

"I didn't see anything," she began. "It's like I told the police, the person came up from behind me." She touched her hand to the bandage on the side of her head. "They hit me with something and then ran off."

"Is that where they hit you? Not the back?" Anne asked.

"Yeah. I heard a noise and started to turn, but it was too late. I got hit and fell down and scraped my hands." She held them up to show Anne the bandages. "Then the guy ran off, and that's the last thing I remember."

"Guy?"

Talia fidgeted in the bed. "I guess it could've been a girl. I'm not sure which."

"That's okay," Anne assured her quickly. "Where were you when it happened?"

"Outside the hospital. I was heading to my car."

"What time was that?"

"About nine."

Surprised, Anne angled her head. "That was pretty late for you to be leaving the studio, wasn't it?"

"I know." Fresh tears welled in her eyes. She swallowed hard and lowered her gaze to her hands, which were tightly clasped in her lap. "I stayed to clean up and…you know…start a load of laundry. All those gloves." She looked up at Anne, her eyes wide and frightened. "I know that's much later than any of the previous attacks. Do you think the mugger was waiting for me?"

"I really couldn't say."

Something was off. Anne couldn't say what it was or how she knew, but she felt it in her gut. She licked her lips and changed tactics.

"Talia, I was thinking about your necklace this morning, the one you told me came from the Bahamas."

Her chin lifted a smidge. "Yeah?"

"Can I see it?"

Her hand fluttered to her bare neck and back to her lap. "I left it in my locker. The clasp has been giving me trouble."

Anne nodded. "Yes, I remember you saying that. Do you mind telling me where you got it?"

She swallowed and then her lips tightened. Anne might have missed the tiny, almost imperceptible movement if she hadn't been looking for it.

"It was a gift," Talia said, her voice low.

"From Dr. Seybold?"

Talia's face flushed red and she clenched her teeth, making the muscles along her jaw harden and jut. "Is this what you wanted my help with? Why you came to see me?"

"Well, I—"

"Marcus didn't attack me," Talia interrupted before Anne could finish. "Sure, we had a fling, and I broke it off, but he would never do something like this. Not unless…" She touched the bandage again, only this time she also bit her lip as though she was troubled.

"Talia, what is it?"

She blinked and turned her focus to Anne. "I was just thinking about last night. The police found something in the bushes where the attack took place."

This was new. Anne sat up straighter in her chair. "Did you see it? Do you have any idea what it was?"

Talia reached up to grab her ponytail and ran the ends of it through her fingers. "I mean, I didn't get a clear look at it but…I kinda thought it might have been a lab coat. It was dirty though, like it had been there a long time. At least a week," she clarified.

"Dr. Seybold is missing a lab coat," Anne said carefully. Marilyn had made it clear he liked to wear one outside of the hospital to enhance his doctor persona, but would he have been so careless as to leave it behind after one of the attacks?

"It couldn't be Marcus's, right?" This time, Talia didn't sound so certain. She gripped the edge of the blanket and pulled it up around her shoulders. "Besides, what about your friend?"

"You mean Shirley?"

Talia nodded, a move that should have made her wince in pain but didn't. "She never dated Marcus. Why would he attack her?"

Anne had already been over that with Ralph. She knew about a possible motive there but didn't say so. She didn't have to. Marcus wasn't the mugger. In fact, unless she missed her mark, the person behind the attacks, the one who'd injured Shirley and Nora and the others…

The mugger was lying in the bed in front of her.

Chapter Twenty-Nine

ANNE FIDGETED FROM FOOT TO foot while she waited for Seamus and Garrison to unlock the door to the fitness studio. Finally, the lock clicked and the door swung open.

"Now, what are we looking for again?" Garrison asked, feeling along the wall until he came to the light switch. He flicked it on, flooding the room in the bluish glow of the fluorescent lights.

"It's back here, next to the restrooms." Anne motioned toward the rear of the studio then led the way. "I carried all of our gloves to the laundry bin and dumped them in, but one fell behind and I pulled it out."

She stopped. As she suspected, the laundry bin had been moved, the telltale dust streaks on the floor showing just where it had been shoved aside and replaced. "Thank goodness Benny was assigned to this room. He never bothered to sweep behind the bin."

Seamus crouched down for a closer look at the streak marks. "It certainly looks like it was shoved around a bit."

"More than once when Anne moved it to get to the glove?" Garrison asked.

Seamus nodded and pointed to several scuffs going side to side and not front and back as Anne had described. "Looks like she got a little desperate when she couldn't find the shirt."

"She saw the dust streaks on the floor when she came back to empty the bin," Anne said quietly. "She knew someone had found the shirt and had to do something to speed up her plan."

"Which was?" Garrison scratched his head. "Sorry, but I'm still not following."

Seamus stood. "I think what Anne is trying to say is she thinks Talia was trying to frame someone for the attacks."

"That's correct, and I think I know who." Anne pointed to the lockers. "One more thing. Can we check Talia's locker for her necklace? She said she left it there, but I have a sneaking suspicion we won't find it."

Seamus nodded and moved toward the lockers, which had combination locks built into the doors.

As Anne took a closer look, though, she realized that Talia's locker wasn't closed all the way. Something was caught in the corner.

She reached for the handle and tugged.

The locker opened, but the only thing in there was a sweatshirt.

Seamus grabbed the sweatshirt and checked the pockets before taking a flashlight from the belt at his waist and shining it around inside the locker. "Nothing." He tossed the sweatshirt back in the locker, then flicked off his flashlight and turned to Anne. "How did you know the necklace wouldn't be in there?"

"Talia said the clasp was loose. I think it was damaged the night Susan Merchant was attacked."

"But that doesn't explain where it is now," Garrison said.

"I haven't seen it again since Nora was attacked outside the hospital," Anne explained. "We might want to start looking there."

She explained what the security team would be looking for, and then Seamus snatched up his radio to bark instructions. That done, he looked at Anne. "What made you remember the necklace?"

Anne shrugged. "Well, it was Talia, actually. She admitted Dr. Seybold gave it to her, but then she went on to say she was the one who broke things off between them. Earlier, she claimed she didn't want anything to do with him, but if that was true, why would she go on wearing the gift he gave her?"

"I guess it'll be easy enough to get his side of things," Garrison said, then shook his head. "I suspected there was something going on between them. I'd heard rumors. But with Marcus, that wasn't uncommon, and I didn't think it fair to hold it against Talia."

"So you hired her anyway."

He nodded, and Anne thought back to that moment in Garrison's office when he'd appeared troubled at the mention of Talia's class. He wore the same look now.

Anne touched his arm. "You couldn't have known she would carry things this far."

He ducked his head in gratitude. "I appreciate that, Anne. Thank you." He drew in a deep breath and looked at Seamus. "I think it would be prudent to post someone outside Talia's door while your guys are looking for the necklace. Also, we need to call your contact at the police department. They're going to want to be in on this."

"Try Officer Carson," Anne said. "He has the shirt we found. We took it to him last night."

"I'll take care of it," Seamus said, moving off to one side to place the call.

Anne looked at Garrison. "Also, someone should look at Talia's hands. She probably tried to cover the old wound with some new ones, but the nurse who was on duty could probably tell us if she was successful."

"You're right. I'll take care of that right now."

Anne caught him before he could move off. "While you and Seamus are taking care of those things, would you mind if I called Shirley and the others? They should know what is going on."

"Of course not. Go right ahead. I'm sure it'll be a relief to Shirley to know the mugger is in custody. At least, she will be soon, thanks to you."

"Thanks to all of us," Anne corrected. "All of us working together."

Garrison smiled but said nothing. While he went to make his phone calls, Anne took out her cell and made hers. Shirley was, of course, relieved and eager to let Regina know the mugger had been caught so she could finally quit worrying about her daughter. Evelyn and Joy were already on their way to the hospital for work and offered to meet Anne when she spoke to the police, but with nothing really final until Talia was actually in custody, Anne didn't think it necessary. She had just hung up when Seamus jogged back to them, his radio in his hand and a look of worry causing creases to form across his brow.

Anne's heart leapt to her throat. "Seamus, what is it? What's wrong?" But deep down, she knew what he'd say before he said it. A second later, he opened his mouth and confirmed what she feared.

"It's Talia," he said. "The guys checked her room. I'm sorry, Anne. She's gone."

Chapter Thirty

"WHAT DO YOU MEAN SHE'S gone?" Garrison snapped before Anne could reply. He planted his hands on his hips, a dark scowl making his face thunderous. "Didn't anyone see her leave?"

Seamus held up the radio. "It doesn't sound like it. The security team is questioning the nursing staff now and checking the security cameras, but apparently she slipped out without anyone noticing."

"That's possible," Anne said. "No one was around when I went up to her room."

Seamus glanced at Anne. "How long ago did you talk to her?"

She looked at her watch. It had taken her a while to catch Seamus before his shift ended, and then they'd had to wait until Garrison arrived before heading down the studio. "It's been over an hour," she said, her shoulders drooping. "She could be anywhere by now."

"Okay, let's think. Do we know where she lives?" Seamus asked.

"We could pull it from HR," Garrison said. "I'm sure there's an address for her on file."

"Do that." Seamus turned to Anne. "Did Talia say anything to you when you left…anything that might give us a clue about where she'd be going?"

Anne mentally reviewed their conversation but shook her head. "No, I'm sorry, Seamus. She didn't say a thing—" She stopped, and her mouth fell open as a terrible thought struck.

Seamus laid his hand on her arm. "Anne? What is it?"

She turned widened eyes to him. "Surely...Talia wouldn't..."

"Anne." Seamus gave her arm a slight shake. "If you're thinking something, you need to tell us."

"Yes." Garrison stepped closer. "Do you think you know where she might have gone?"

"It's just a hunch, really."

"At this point, I think we're all ready to listen to your hunches." Garrison urged her on. "Go ahead."

"Well, it just occurred to me...when does Dr. Seybold get to the hospital? I know he goes running every day at the same time. Is he just as consistent with his arrival?"

Both men looked at her in surprise.

"I'm not..." Garrison lifted one hand and shrugged. "I really couldn't say. Do you think Talia went to talk to him?"

"Maybe not talk," Anne said, a shudder traveling her spine. "If I'm right, and Talia is our culprit, she's been hanging on to one of Marcus's lab coats. Last night, she planted it outside the hospital to make him look guilty of attacking her. I realize that probably wasn't her original plan, but still."

"You think she's escalating." Seamus said it matter-of-factly, with no doubt in his voice to make Anne question her theory. She nodded. Seamus looked at Garrison. "What time?"

Garrison looked at his own watch. "He should be arriving any minute."

"Does he use the parking garage?" Seamus was already reaching for his radio.

"Yeah, far as I know." Garrison looked at Anne. "We should get over there."

Anne started moving as he said it, both Garrison and Seamus close on her heels. As they got closer, she slowed.

"What's wrong?" Seamus asked.

Anne gestured toward the walkways visible through the lobby windows. "Ground level or second floor? There are two walkways. Which one would he use?"

"His office is on the fourth floor," Garrison said. "Wouldn't he park by the one closest to his office?"

"Maybe, but…" She looked at Seamus.

"I got ya. We'll cover both, just in case." He gave clipped instructions into the radio then motioned Anne forward. "Let's go."

"What kind of car does Dr. Seybold drive?" Anne asked, slightly out of breath and huffing by the time they reached the parking garage.

Garrison also looked winded. "I have no idea. Seamus?"

He shook his head. Fortunately, there weren't many cars filling the spaces this early in the morning. The smell of exhaust wafted on the air. Mixed with the colder temperatures, they formed a gray cloud that seemed to hover over the cement walls and floor. It made the entire scene eerily quiet.

Anne scanned the rows to her right and then to her left. "Maybe we should split up."

Seamus hitched his thumb to the left. "I'll go this way. Garrison, you and Anne check the other way. Do either of you have a phone in case you spot her?"

"Good thinking." Anne tugged her phone from her pocket.

Garrison did the same then touched Anne's elbow. "Let's go." To Seamus, he said, "Be careful."

"You too." He took off at a jog, his footstep echoing along the cold walls.

Anne sucked in a breath. "Garrison, do you think maybe we should have tried calling Dr. Seybold to warn him or something?"

"That's not a bad idea."

"Have you got his number?"

"No, but I can get it." He jabbed the buttons on his phone, listened a moment, then spoke to Julie, his tone low and urgent. After a moment, he hung up and showed the phone to Anne. "Got it."

"Okay, you call his number and keep calling until you get him."

"We can do that and walk at the same time."

Anne nodded. Several times, Garrison hit the redial key on his phone as they wound up and down through the rows until they neared the end. A ways off, Seamus had rounded the corner and was working his way back toward them.

And then Anne heard it. Distant ringing. Compounded by distance and the echo created by the cement, it was hard to tell which way it was coming from. She grabbed Garrison's arm. "Stop."

"What?"

"Listen." They froze, both of them searching for the direction of the sound. Seamus also halted in his tracks. Her hand shaking, Anne pointed. Just a few rows down, Dr. Seybold stood in the middle of the lane, deep in conversation with Talia. But what he couldn't see from his angle, what he didn't know was that behind her back, she clutched something long and rigid. Something black.

Anne sucked in a breath. Talia clutched a tire iron, and by the way she was easing toward Dr. Seybold, she looked like she had every intention of using it on him.

Chapter Thirty-One

"MARCUS, DUCK! LOOK OUT!" GARRISON yelled, waving his hand over his head.

Seamus was a blur. He leaped into the lane and ran, arms pumping, and hit Talia broadside, knocking her to the ground just as she brought her arm forward to swing at Marcus's head.

Anne opened her mouth, but no scream came out. Though she knew she should move, her feet stayed frozen to the cement floor. Somewhere close, she heard sirens.

"Anne? Anne!"

Slowly, Garrison's face came into focus. He gripped her by the arms and gave her a shake. "I have to help Seamus. Will you be all right?"

"I'm fine. Go," she said. He whirled and was gone in almost the same instant. She could breathe now. And think. "Marcus."

Remembering Dr. Seybold, Anne turned to look for him. Though he was pale, he appeared otherwise unhurt—a statement that might not have been true had Seamus been slower to respond. Anne hurried toward him. "Are you okay?"

Dr. Seybold nodded. It was then that Anne noticed that Seamus was still on the ground, wincing in pain and holding his wrist. She rushed to him and grasped his upper arm. "I'm going to call for help. Try not to move."

"What about Talia?" Seamus asked through clenched teeth.

She twisted to look. Garrison had kicked the tire iron from Talia's reach and now helped her to her feet, one hand firmly on her arm. "Garrison has her."

Anne reached for her phone, but in fact, she didn't have to call. People had heard the commotion and notified medical personnel, who already rushed through the walkway toward them. Anne backed out of their way as they drew closer. Seamus was in good hands. So was Dr. Seybold. Despite almost being struck over the head, he looked his usual charming self as he was led away by a nurse. Anne tore her gaze away. Did he even realize how close he'd come to being seriously injured…or worse?

She shook her head and went to join Garrison. Next to him, Talia stood sullen and defeated, her shoulders slumped, as though all the fire had drained from her and all that was left was a sad, broken woman.

Anne approached her carefully. "Are you all right, Talia?"

She lifted her chin and didn't answer.

"I understand. You don't have to talk to me if you don't want to. I just wish you would tell me why." Anne spread her hands wide. "Why all this?"

Slowly, the resolve Talia had found crumbled, and she turned pain-filled eyes to Anne. "You don't know? I assumed you'd figured it out when you asked about the necklace." She shuddered and dropped her gaze. "It was to get back at Marcus."

Swiping her finger under her eyes, she said, "He made promises, talked about our future together. That's how he convinced me to go with him to the Bahamas. I thought we'd get married...start a family. Instead, he left me after we got back—dropped me for another woman almost as soon as our plane landed. I was angry and hurt. I wanted to lash out at him. I thought if I could make people think he was the one attacking people, his reputation and his career would be ruined."

"But you hurt people, Talia. *Innocent* people," Garrison said.

She looked up, her jaw hardening. "Did anyone care that I was hurt? Did anyone ask me if I was okay?"

Her reasoning was flawed, but blinded by her own pain, she couldn't see it. Anne sighed. "So you planned out your attacks knowing the timing would cast suspicion on Dr. Seybold."

"Yes, that's what I did."

Police officers had arrived. Anne stepped back as they took Talia into custody. She and Garrison would likely have to repeat everything they'd heard, but that was minor compared to the criminal charges Talia would face.

Poor Talia. Anne couldn't help but feel sorry for someone so lost and desperate.

"Anne!"

Above the din of sirens and emergency personnel, her name echoed off the parking garage walls. Turning a slow circle to look for the source, she saw Evelyn and Joy hurrying toward her. Both looked aghast with shock and worry.

"Are you okay?" Joy demanded, grabbing Anne's arm.

She grinned. "Wow. Tight grip. Those workout classes you've been taking must really be working."

"Don't joke," Evelyn said, her face stern, but when Joy laughed with relief, and then Anne, she relented a bit and smiled. "So is it true?" She motioned to the growing crowd forming around them. "People are saying Talia tried to attack Dr. Seybold with a tire iron."

"It's true." Anne nodded and rubbed a sudden chill from her arms. "If it hadn't been for Seamus, she might have done it."

Anne took a moment to explain all that had happened leading up to the place they now stood, then clapped her hand over her forehead. "Oh my goodness…I have to call Ralph and Shirley before they hear about this from someone else."

"You call Ralph. I'll call Shirley," Joy offered.

Anne made the call and then motioned toward an officer who was placing Talia in handcuffs.

"What a pity. She's such a bright, promising young woman. I wish we could have helped her." Fighting a swell of remorse, Anne looked over at Evelyn.

Evelyn slid her arm around Anne's shoulder and hugged her tight. A few minutes later, Ralph did the same on Anne's other side.

"You okay, sweetheart?"

Bookended by two of the people she loved most, and joined a few seconds later by a third as Joy returned to them, Anne could say yes. But Talia…

A police car rolled past with the young woman in the back seat, her eyes closed and face pale.

Garrison walked toward the spot where Anne and her friends stood. "How's Shirley?"

His concern warmed Anne's heart. He cared deeply for Shirley, and she for him.

"She knows," Joy said, patting her pocket. "I just got off the phone with her."

Relief flooded his face. "Good."

"What about Talia?" Anne asked. "Will she be all right?"

"Her wounds will heal in time." Garrison sighed and jammed his hands into the pockets of his lab coat. "Her mental state will take a lot longer to evaluate."

"And to think, all this time, we were talking about the attacks in front of her. Maybe even feeding her information about added security and possible suspects." Anne shuddered and rubbed her hands over her arms again.

"So I assume she really did use the CrossFit gloves to hide the wound from Susan's keys?" Evelyn asked.

"I think so." Anne nodded. "But we probably won't know for sure until the police have a chance to take another look at her hands."

"But then what about the schedule?" Joy asked. "She couldn't have known she would need the gloves."

"No, but she was able to make adjustments using an app on her phone," Anne said. "She must have changed the schedule when she noticed the laundry bin had been moved."

"Which is probably why you didn't remember seeing it," Evelyn finished.

"So many signs." Anne breathed a deep sigh. "And to think we almost missed them."

"This wasn't your fault, sweetheart," Ralph said. "Once you realized what was going on, you did a good job of putting the pieces together to stop Talia. Thank goodness there will be no more attacks on innocent Mercy employees."

"And at least now, she'll be able to get the help she needs," Joy said. "That's something."

Yes, it was something, and yet…

For the hurting world they lived in, it wasn't enough. And Anne deeply wished it could be more.

Chapter Thirty-Two

A FEW DAYS LATER, A cheer went up from the nurses' station when Shirley stepped onto the floor dressed in scrubs instead of her street clothes. Flanked by Evelyn and Joy, Anne cheered along. It felt good to see her friend moving back into her role at the hospital, especially now that Preston's attorney had convinced him to drop all the medical malpractice suits and enroll himself in grief counseling. Last Anne heard, his wife had even agreed to go with him, in a move that she hoped would lead to healing and reconciliation.

When the din calmed down, and after everyone had their chance to welcome their colleague back, Anne held out her hands to clasp Shirley's. "Well, well, well. I must say, you look good in that outfit."

"I couldn't agree more." Joy grinned wickedly and pretended to look Shirley over from head to toe. "Have you lost weight?"

Shirley laughed. "Ha. If I have, it's because I haven't been eating those cafeteria hamburgers. Mama has put us both on a high-protein, low-carb regimen."

Joy's face suddenly turned serious. "I'll have to ask her for some recipes."

"Forget about that," Anne joked and let go of Shirley's hands. She lowered her voice. "What we really want to know is if the rumors about Garrison thinking about proposing to a certain someone we know are true."

"Um…" Shrinking under their gaze, Shirley pressed her hands to her face. "I mean, he did say he had something he wanted to talk to me about the next time we go out."

Anne cut short a squeal. Next to her, Evelyn did the same. "It's about time he realized what a great catch he has in front of him," she said.

The elevator dinged and Garrison got off, making his way toward them, a beautiful bouquet of flowers in his hand.

"Hey, Shirley. Welcome back."

"Thank you." She cleared her throat and motioned toward the flowers. "Are those for me?"

He held the flowers toward her, his hand covering hers as she took them and lingering there while he looked into her eyes.

"We'll…just…" Joy fanned her face then cast about for help from either Anne or Evelyn.

"Let's give them a moment," Anne finished for her.

Evelyn's head bobbed so hard she knocked a lock of hair askew. "Yeah, let's. We can talk over by the elevators where it's quiet. Come on, girls."

Taking each of them by the elbow, she pulled them briskly away from Garrison and Shirley, but it was her sigh that was the loudest when she saw Garrison lift his hand to touch the side of Shirley's face.

"That's so sweet."

"Um, Evelyn? A little privacy?" Joy snatched her arm and whirled her around so her back was to them. "Besides, don't you have some catching up to do now that your computer's fixed?"

"Yes, but—"

"No buts. Let's go." Joy punched the button for the elevator, her face comically stern.

Watching them, Anne chuckled. She loved her funny, quirky, problem-solving friends. Between them and her family, she had so much to be thankful for, even if she had been holding on to them a little too tight in recent weeks.

Inside the elevator car, Joy gave her a nudge with her elbow. "Whatcha thinking about?"

The doors slid shut, closing out one final glimpse of Garrison and Shirley as he took her hand.

"Actually, I was just thinking about how happy I am to have all of you in my life." Anne lifted one hand and began counting each of them off on her fingers. "You, Evelyn, Shirley, Ralph...you're always there whenever something is going on with Lili or Addie. I know I don't say it enough, but I'm so thankful to have friends I can count on no matter what the circumstances."

For a moment, no one spoke, and then Joy took one of her hands and Evelyn the other. "It meant the world to me having you three by my side. I was very lonely after Wilson passed away," Joy said. "You three helped fill that void. If I never told you that, I'm sorry."

"You've told us, but I agree with Anne. We can't say it too often," Evelyn said, her low tone matching Joy's. "I guess I never realized how lucky we are to have each other until Shirley—" She broke off, cleared her throat, and started again. "After Shirley was attacked, I just felt like I'd been taking the three of you always being here for granted."

"I felt the same way." Compelled by a twinge of guilt, Anne added, "Well, if I'm honest, it went a little deeper than that, but I'm over it now, thanks to some help from above."

She smiled, knowing that her loving Father had forgiven…and would always forgive her…for her moments of faithlessness and fear.

She sniffled, and her gaze encompassed both her friends. "But I won't make that mistake again, because you mean the world to me. And no matter what…"

Looking first at Joy and then Evelyn, she held up their hands and shook them. "Besides my family, you two and Shirley will always be the most important people in my life. I'll never stop being thankful for our friendship."

"Neither will I," Joy said.

"Or me," Evelyn added.

"Good, then that's settled. And I'm glad because…" A slow grin spread over Anne's face. "Going after bad guys who attack my friends is exhausting."

Dear Reader,

My family spent a lot of time in hospitals during the writing of this book, first with my father, who passed away in January; my granddaughter, who was born in April after a difficult pregnancy; and then with my husband, who had to have hip surgery after years of putting up with pain. In a way, my journey over the past twelve months so closely resembled Anne's that I found myself crying and closing my computer when the story hit too close to home. It's hard trusting God with our loved ones! Even though I know He cares for them far better than I can, writing about Anne's struggle reminded me that we are all human and subject to crises of faith. Thankfully, our Father is patient and able to bear with us in all our seasons of doubt. I pray this book offers you encouragement, dear reader, and that you find yourself comforted by the knowledge that God is faithful, even when we are not.

Signed,
Elizabeth Ludwig

About the Author

ELIZABETH LUDWIG IS A *USA Today*-bestselling author whose work has been featured on Novel Rocket, More to Life Magazine, and Christian Fiction Online Magazine. She is an accomplished speaker and teacher, often attending conferences and seminars where she lectures on editing for fiction writers, crafting effective novel proposals, and conducting successful editor/agent interviews. Her first novel, *Where the Truth Lies*, which she coauthored with Janelle Mowery, earned her the IWA Writer of the Year Award. Her second novel, *Died in the Wool*, also coauthored with Janelle Mowery, was nominated for a Carol Award.

In 2012, her Edge of Freedom series released from Bethany House Publishers. Books one and two, *No Safe Harbor* and *Dark Road Home*, respectively, earned 4 Stars from RT Book Reviews. Book three in the series, *Tide and Tempest*, received top honors with 4½ Stars and was named a finalist for the Gayle Wilson Award of Excellence.

Elizabeth was also honored to be awarded a HOLT Medallion in 2018 for her book *A Tempting Taste of Mystery*, part of the Sugarcreek Amish Mysteries series from Guideposts. Most recently, she was named a dual-finalist in the 2020 Selah Awards for her novella "In Hot Water," part of the bestselling collection *The Coffee Club*

Mysteries from Barbour Publishing, and *Garage Sale Secret*, part of the Mysteries of Lancaster County series from Guideposts. Her latest release, "Christmas in Galway," part of the *Christmas Lights and Romance* collection from Winged Publications, was a finalist for the 2021 Carol Award.

Along with her husband and children, Elizabeth makes her home in the great state of Texas. To learn more, sign up for her newsletter at ElizabethLudwig.com or visit her on Facebook.

An Armchair Tour of Charleston

October is a wonderful time of year to visit Charleston, but anytime is a great time to buy a ticket for the Black Fedora Comedy Mystery Theater. Located one block from the City Market on Church Street, the Black Fedora Theater is a small venue that seats sixty guests most nights for crazy comical mysteries and delicious homemade appetizers and desserts.

Choosing which play you want to see at the Black Fedora is no easy task. Do you want to see *Inspector No Clue*, the theater's longest-running play, which features the Man in the Black Fedora, who is "one part Bogart, one part Holmes, and two parts Clouseau"? Or maybe you'll choose *Sherlock's Other Brother by a Southern Mother*. How about *Redneck Reunion*, "where Grandpa is off his meds, Ruby Jewel insists on singing, there's that dead body stuck up under the tater table, and Crazy Cousin Carl is...well, he's just crazy"?

All of the Black Fedora's plays are rated G or PG—there's never any bad language or crude subject matter—and everyone age seven and up is welcome. You can even volunteer to be in the play! They'll give you a script and let you ham it up to your heart's content. As one customer said in his review, "Don't worry about being Meryl Streep or Dustin Hoffman, because whether audience performers are good or bad is completely beside the point. You'll be laughing too hard at the whole setup to care."

If you're planning a trip to Charleston, be sure to book yourself a night at the Black Fedora Comedy Mystery Theater. It'll be a rollicking two hours of laughter and hijinks, and don't forget to try the Fatal Fudge Volcano Cake!

Good for What Ails You

Regina's Fudgy Mayo Brownies

Ingredients:

¾ cup all-purpose flour

1 teaspoon baking powder

½ teaspoon salt

1 cup sugar

½ cup mayonnaise

2 eggs

1 teaspoon vanilla extract

1 cup semisweet chocolate chips

½ cup chopped walnuts

Directions:

Heat oven to 350°F. Combine flour, baking powder, and salt in a small bowl; set aside.

Spray an 8-inch square baking pan with nonstick cooking spray or line with aluminum foil; set aside.

In a large bowl, combine sugar, mayonnaise, eggs, and vanilla; stir until smooth and set aside.

Place chocolate chips in a double boiler, heat over medium heat for 3 minutes or until chocolate is melted, stirring often.

Stir egg mixture into melted chocolate until smooth.

Stir flour mixture and walnuts into chocolate batter until blended.

Spread batter into prepared baking pan.

Bake on center oven rack for 35 minutes or until a toothpick inserted 1 inch from the edge comes out clean.

Place pan of brownies on a wire rack and cool.

Cut brownies into 16 squares and serve.

Read on for a sneak peek of another exciting book in the Sweet Carolina Mysteries series!

Ill at Ease

BY JANICE THOMPSON

EVELYN PERRY GRABBED A TRAY and made her way to the hot foods section of Mercy Hospital's cafeteria. Today's special—grilled chicken breast with a side of green beans—was her favorite. And with only thirty minutes for her lunch break, she needed something healthy to fuel her afternoon.

Three people stood in line ahead of her—a tall man, a petite elderly woman, and a woman just ahead of her with beautiful auburn hair.

The auburn-haired woman ahead of her had on a gorgeous embroidered jacket. It looked expensive. She also wore high heels with her jeans, something Evelyn would never attempt, at least not on a typical workday. She'd stick to her flats. Heels wouldn't do for walking back and forth to the hospital from her home in Charleston's beautiful historic district.

On the other side of the counter, a familiar young woman with a sloppy ponytail waited on the customers, moving at record speed.

Evelyn didn't know Avery well, but their paths had crossed the year before when Avery's husband agreed to sit on the board for the hospital's museum. Of course, that was before Collier's cancer diagnosis, the one that had taken his life only a few brief months ago.

Evelyn had been praying for Avery and her kids since receiving the news.

Avery looked tired today. From the downward slope of her lips and the fine lines around her eyes, it would appear she needed a good night's sleep. Or maybe some good news?

Evelyn hoped to give her something to smile about.

In the meantime, the woman in front of her made small talk with Avery about the chilly weather. "I walked here this morning from my place on Church Street," she explained. "But I don't really mind. It's not that far."

Avery's eyes widened. "You live on Church Street? Wow."

"I do." The pitch of the woman's voice rose a bit. "Do you know it?"

Evelyn wanted to say "Who doesn't?" but didn't. Church Street boasted some of Charleston's finest houses, after all. Many of them dated back to the Civil War. Their stories were legendary. Many had not survived the fires. Others had risen from the ashes, restored to new life.

"You live in one of those big, fancy houses?" Avery's gaze shifted to the woman and then down to the food she was serving, and she muttered, "Must be nice."

"Yes and no," the woman said. "The house was built in the 1700s. It takes a lot of work to maintain something that old."

Evelyn couldn't help herself. She had to toss in a few thoughts on the matter. "I'm in an older house not far from Church Street, so I get it."

"Oh, you're in the historic district too?" The woman glanced over her shoulder at Evelyn. With her face almost in full view, she looked familiar but Evelyn couldn't figure out where she'd seen her before. The woman seemed to recognize her too. She froze in place, eyes narrowed as she took her in.

"Yes." Evelyn nodded as she nudged her tray up a few inches. "I grew up there. But our home was no showcase. When you're dealing with a house that old, you've got all kinds of problems."

"Exactly. That's my point." The woman paused to order a chef salad then turned back to face her.

Evelyn had that same feeling all over again, that she knew her.

"My place on Church Street is over 275 years old, and you don't even want to know all we've been through to keep it up and running." The woman paused to adjust her purse strap. "It's a lot to handle."

Evelyn knew exactly where she meant. "Wow," she said. "You're in Chadwick House." It happened to be one of the finest in the city.

"Yes. I married into it, I guess you could say." The woman offered a tiny shrug, and a hint of moisture glistened in her eyes. "I would give it all back just to have my husband well again."

From behind the counter, Avery dissolved into tears. She set the salad bowl down and bolted from the area, leaving no one to wait on them.

"Oh my. What did I say?" The woman lifted her hands to her throat as she glanced Evelyn's way.

"You didn't say anything wrong," Evelyn assured her as she shifted her gaze to the other side of the counter, to the empty space where Avery once stood. "She's going through a hard time right now."

"Well, I certainly understand that. I'm Julianna, by the way." The woman extended her hand, a magnificent diamond ring casting a brilliant shimmer and shine.

"Wait…Julianna Harrison?" Evelyn stared, now realizing that she did know her after all. "Did you go to Charleston Southern?"

"Sure did. But it's Julianna Chadwick now." Julianna's eyes narrowed, and her heavily painted lips tipped up in a smile. She placed her hand on her hips. "Wait a minute…Evie?"

Evelyn laughed. "I love that you still call me that, Juli."

"Guilty as charged." Julianna's smile deepened. "And you're one of the few who still calls me Juli. Everyone else knows me as Julianna. I can't believe it's you! After all these years!"

"I thought you moved away."

"Oh, I did. That's a long story." Julianna gestured to a nearby table. "Do you have a few minutes for lunch? My husband is—" She shook her head. "Anyway, he won't miss me. And I need the distraction, trust me. It's been a rough ride, of late."

Evelyn nodded. "And now that you say that, I remember filing records for a Chadwick a week or so ago. He was in an accident?"

"Yes." Julianna's eyes grew moist. "Just over a week ago." Her voice cracked with emotion. "It was terrible. He was hit by the driver of a semi who fell asleep at the wheel."

"I'm so sorry. My good friend is married to the chaplain, and she asked me to pray for him."

"Ralph Mabry. Is that who you mean?"

"Yes, his wife, Anne, has volunteered at Mercy Hospital for thirty years, and Ralph is our resident chaplain."

"Oh, I know." Julianna's lips tipped up in a smile. "I can't tell you how many times I've called on Ralph to pray for Charles over the past week. I met Anne in passing one day when she dropped off some flowers in my husband's room. They're both great people."

"They are." Evelyn rested a hand on Julianna's arm. "I'm so very sorry about your husband. How is he doing?"

"He's in a medically induced coma. They're saying…" Julianna shook her head. "They're saying he might have brain damage, which is why they've left him sleeping for so long, to allow time for the swelling to go down and to get the bleeding under control." Fine lines formed between her eyes as she lowered her voice to add, "It's a frightening time, Evie. So many unknowns. I never thought I'd go through something like this. But then again, I don't suppose anyone ever does."

"I'm so sorry." Evelyn wasn't sure what else to say.

"I refuse to believe that I might lose him. I just can't even…" Julianna's words trailed off.

From behind them in line, a couple of customers began to grumble about the lack of service. Evelyn didn't blame them. She glanced around. "Tell you what. Let me go fetch the manager so we can get our food. Then we can find a table and catch up."

Relief flooded Juli's face. "You have no idea how much I would love that."

"Perfect." Evelyn located the manager, and he finished filling their order, prepping the chef's salad for Julianna and loading a plate with grilled chicken and green beans for Evelyn.

"Please excuse Avery." The manager leaned in close, his voice lowered as he passed the food their way. "She's still mourning."

"Mourning?" Julianna looked confused.

"Yes, she recently lost her husband," Evelyn explained. "He was a wonderful young man."

"This has been a hard time for her," the manager said. "Especially with the holidays coming. I know she's worried about the kids."

"Oh no!" Julianna pressed a hand to her heart. "That's just awful. And I had to go and put my foot in my mouth with that comment about wishing my husband was well."

"You couldn't have known." Evelyn turned to face the manager. "I've been praying for her. Please let her know."

He nodded. "I will. I haven't known what to say or do. She's got two kids—a boy and a girl. This is going to be such a hard season for them, losing their dad and all. And now she's about to lose her house too. They're really struggling."

Evelyn waited until her friend took a seat, then offered to fill their glasses at the drink station.

While she was waiting in line, a couple of men entered the cafeteria. They were a bit rough around the edges with messy hair and clothes that looked wrinkled and faded. One was slightly taller than the other and wore a plaid shirt and jeans with a baseball cap. The other was in a T-shirt and grimy jeans. He was balding on top, but had a full mustache. They shared a lot of features in common, and she guessed they must be brothers.

She probably wouldn't have paid them much mind, but one of them pointed to Julianna and said something to the other. Julianna didn't seem to notice them as they got into the line to order food.

After filling the drinks, Evelyn settled into her seat and noticed that Avery was back at work behind the counter with a strained expression on her weary face. Julianna picked at her food, her gaze shifting to Avery as well. "We have to do something for her."

"What do you mean?"

"I'm just saying, if Charles pulls through this…" Julianna tipped her head from side to side, as if weighing her options.

"*When* he pulls through this."

"When Charles pulls through this, I'm going to help that family. I don't know how, but I feel so strongly that I should. It is the holidays, after all. Thanksgiving is coming, and that young woman needs hope." She paused to dab at her nose with her napkin. "We all do."

"Yes, we do. And that would be lovely, Juli. Maybe we can work on a plan."

"Yes, let's. It'll be like old times, with you organizing the effort." She smiled. "You always were the organizer."

Evelyn returned her smile. "Still am." She cut a bite of her chicken. "So, you're Julianna Chadwick now, not Harrison."

"Yes." Julianna opened her dressing packet. "But there was another last name between those two. Sawyer. I married right out of college and it lasted twenty-seven years. I got two great kids out of that union before Karl passed. They're grown and living elsewhere now."

"Oh my. I'm so sorry to hear that. About your husband, I mean."

Julianna's nose wrinkled. "My life has had a lot of twists and turns since I saw you last, Evie. It's a mixed bag, for sure."

"I'm sure that was very hard."

"Oh, it was. And"—she lowered her voice—"Karl left me with so much debt. He was one of those entrepreneur types, always coming up with a way to make money. Only he rarely did. But I loved him dearly, in spite of it."

Out of the corner of her eye, Evelyn caught a glimpse of the two men she'd seen earlier. They settled in at the table right next to theirs.

Julianna glanced their way and smiled. They waved, and she did the same. Just as quickly, though, her smile faded. "It wasn't a good financial situation when I was married to Karl, that's for sure. After he passed, there were months I didn't know if I would be able to pay rent on our little house in Atlanta. But I kept working—at the bank, by the way—and one day this handsome customer came in and struck up a conversation." Her eyes lit up. "He was in Atlanta on business. Charles owns Chadwick Investments."

"Yes, I've heard of that."

"I didn't know him from Adam. But, next thing you know, he's asking me out on a date." Julianna giggled.

"Sounds exciting."

"It was." She released a contented sigh, and Evelyn could see the joy in her eyes. "I know my coworkers thought I was crazy, going out with a man so much older than I am. I mean, fifteen years is a bit of a gap, especially when you're getting up there."

"You still look so young, Juli."

"Well, I meant him, not me, but thank you. I try." She dabbed her lips with her napkin.

Some folks didn't have to try too hard, though. Julianna had always been a real beauty with her creamy skin and a tiny splattering of freckles on her nose.

A dreamy, faraway look came over her. "Charles was—is—just the sweetest guy. So I agreed to meet him for coffee, and things just went from there." Julianna took a sip of her drink and then set it down. "But I wish you could've seen my face when I found out he was *that* Charles Chadwick, the one with the big account at the bank. I almost ran for the hills."

Evelyn smiled. "But you didn't."

Julianna's eyes sparkled. "Well, he was kind of irresistible. Let's just say he knows how to woo a girl. He was always sending little gifts and notes, and he seemed to adore my kids." Julianna grew silent. Her eyes misted over, but just as quickly her expression brightened. "Now, what about *you*?"

Evelyn wanted to answer, but the men at the table next to her lit into an argument that escalated. One of them shoved back his chair, causing a horrible scraping noise. Then he took off toward the drink station, cup in hand.